Creating Competent Communicators

ACTIVITIES FOR TEACHING SPEAKING, LISTENING, AND MEDIA LITERACY IN GRADES 7-12

EDITORS

Pamela Cooper, Ph.D., *Northwestern University*

Sherwyn Morreale, Ph.D., *National Communication Association*

CONTRIBUTORS

Amy Aidman, Ph.D., *University of Illinois*

Melissa Beall, Ph.D., *University of Northern Iowa*

Mary Bozik, Ph.D., *University of Northern Iowa*

Carolyn Coakley, M.A., *International Listening Association*

Arlie Daniel, Ph.D., *East Central University*

Deborah Hefferin, M.A., *Broward Community College*

John Heineman, M.A., *Lincoln High School*

Carolyn Perry, M.A., *National Communication Association*

Gina Marcello-Serafin, *Rutgers, The State University of New Jersey*

In association with The National Communication Association

Holcomb Hathaway, Publishers
Scottsdale, Arizona

Library of Congress Cataloging-in-Publication Data

Creating competent communicators : activities for teaching speaking, listening, and media literacy in grades 7-12 / editors, Pamela J. Cooper, Sherwyn Morreale ; Amy Aidman . . . [et al.] in association with the National Communication Association.
    p. cm.
    Includes bibliographical references.
    ISBN 1-890871-40-0
    1. Oral communication—Study and teaching (Secondary) 2. Media Literacy—Study and teaching (Secondary) I. Cooper, Pamela J. II. Morreale, Sherwyn P. III. Aidman, Amy. IV. National Communication Association (U.S.)

LB1631 .C7217 2003
428'.0071'2—dc21

2002023308

Holcomb Hathaway, Publishers, Inc.
6207 North Cattletrack Road
Scottsdale, Arizona 85250
(480) 991-7881
www.hh-pub.com

10 9 8 7 6 5 4 3 2 1

ISBN 1-890871-40-0

Printed in the United States of America

CONTENTS

"Speaking and listening are to reading and writing what walking is to running."

—Mark Tucker, president, National Center on Education and on the Economy

Unit Four   MEDIA LITERACY   73

Teaching Activities for NCA Standards 16–20

Unit Five   TEACHING RESOURCES   111

PREFACE

The need to address communication education in grades K–12 is a crucial national concern that cannot and should not be ignored. Competence in oral communication—in speaking, listening, and media literacy—is prerequisite to students' personal and academic success in life. In a national review of nearly 100 articles, commentaries, and publications about what graduates must know, four themes emerged that support the importance of communication education: (1) developing the whole person; (2) improving the education enterprise in general; (3) being a responsible citizen of the world; and (4) succeeding in one's career and in the business world. Moreover, oral communication is fundamental to all other learning; a student who cannot communicate may be challenged to learn even the most basic concepts of any other academic discipline.

Despite this need and the establishing of broad sets of language arts objectives by many state departments of education, classroom instruction often still focuses predominantly on reading and writing. As a result, many schools are not educating students in speaking, listening, and media literacy to the extent that they might. However, some state and local accrediting agencies have begun to mandate communication education. In Texas, students are required to take a hybrid communication course. In California, Maryland, and North Carolina, standards programs for all schools significantly include oral communication. Furthermore, such associations as the National Council for Accreditation of Teacher Education and the National Council of Teachers of Mathematics (NCTM) have published new guidelines and standards that include oral communication.

The National Council of Teachers of Mathematics/International Reading Association Standards for the English Language Arts include attention to oral literacy and communication skills. Standard 4 states, "Students adjust their use of spoken, written, and visual language (e.g., conventions, style, vocabulary) to communicate effectively with a variety of audiences and for different purposes."[1] Oral literacy is no longer the sole responsibility of English teachers, as so many educators have believed in the past; efforts must be made to integrate oral language activities across the curriculum. The NCTM's Standard 2 addresses "Mathematics as Communication," saying that students should ". . . be able to reflect upon and clarify their thinking about mathematical ideas and relationships, express mathematical ideas orally and in writing, and ask clarifying and extended questions related to mathematics they have read or heard about."[2] National and state standards for other disciplines make similar claims. Educator Sharon Kane says "Helping our students become skilled listeners and speakers is everyone's job. Welcome the challenge enthusiastically, partly because increased oral literacy can serve to help students reflect on, learn about, and grapple with issues related to all content areas."[3]

Despite small forward movements in teaching communication competence to K–12 students, these steps still inadequately address the field as a whole. For example, teachers may use one formal speaking event, such as an oral report, as the sole measure of a

---

1. NCTE/IRA (1996). *Standards for the English Language Arts,* p. 33.

2. National Council of Teachers of Mathematics (1991). *The Professional Teaching Standards,* p. 140.

3. Sharon Kane. *Content Area Literacy* (2003, in press). Scottsdale, AZ: Holcomb Hathaway.

student's speaking competency. They may teach listening only as an informative process, such as listening to follow directions or to summarize a story. They may have students work in small groups but never discuss how members must communicate to make that small group work effectively and efficiently. They may have students watch a film and discuss its meaning without any prior instruction on the criteria used to evaluate a particular film genre. There may be no instruction at all in nonverbal communication. Such a limited range of content and experiences does not provide adequate instruction in communication.

This inadequate instruction occurs for several reasons. First, many teachers in the public sector incorrectly perceive communication as simply the ability to talk and hear. This narrow concept of communication has caused teachers to underemphasize communication in all its facets. Second, too many educators believe that since children learn to talk and hear naturally, and appear to do it quite well, no further instruction is necessary. Third, educators have traditionally believed that reading and writing skills are highly transferable into oral communication skills. This assumption has been challenged by strong scholarly criticism—the ability to read and write well will not automatically make a student a competent oral communicator. Finally, because language arts teachers (those most likely to be asked to integrate communication instruction into their curricula) have so much to do and so little time, they often neglect a comprehensive approach to teaching the fundamentals of communication, speaking, listening, and media literacy.

Teachers and creators of curriculum are aware of the need to include communication instruction at the K–12, but resources for such instruction have not been available in the past. Most K–12 teachers are convinced of the need to help their students become better communicators, but many remain unprepared or unequipped to do so. As more and more teachers are asked by their state and local departments of education to teach such communication skills as speaking, listening, and media literacy, the need for resources and teaching activities in these areas is becoming blatantly clear.

The National Communication Association (NCA), the world's oldest and largest academic society of communication scholars and teachers, is aware of this problem. In 1995, NCA developed its first set of communication standards for K–12, which were well received across the United States. In 1998, the authors of this book, who have participated for years in K–12 communication activities and publications, revised NCA's first set of standards and added competency statements to enhance their usefulness. The competencies for each standard are statements of expectations regarding what students should know (knowledge), be able to do (behaviors), and be motivated to do (attitudes). This publication of teaching activities now extends the usefulness of NCA's *Competent Communicators: K–12 Speaking, Listening, and Media Literacy Standards and Competency Statements* (1998).

This new activities book introduces the K–12 teacher to communication studies in general and to teaching each of the four components of the NCA standards in particular:

- fundamentals of communication
- speaking
- listening
- media literacy

We provide background information on each of the four components as well as teaching activities for each standard. Any K–12 classroom teacher should be able simply to pick this book up and have the resources to teach communication. This book is, in fact, the only publication available for the K–12 teacher that is grounded in the nationally recognized and disseminated NCA K–12 Speaking, Listening, and Media Literacy Standards and Competencies. It is designed to help those without communication degrees teach a subject in which they are not well trained and teach it comfortably and knowledgeably.

Educators who wish to bring nuance and complexity to their communication instruction approach can use this book with high expectations, not just because of the clear, concise format but, more importantly, because of the scholarship and effort that went into its creation. The authors combined their collective expertise to bring a still-developing field to a new level. The expectations placed on today's students as future citizens of the world to be sophisticated communicators demand nothing less.

Acknowledgments

We would like to thank the following reviewers, who read the manuscript at various stages and offered valuable suggestions for its improvement: Beverly DeVries, Southern Nazarene University; Barbara J. Hall, University of Illinois at Urbana-Champaign; Douglas K. Jennings, Illinois State University; Ruth Kay, Detroit Country Day School; Ginny Reding, Pleasant Hope Middle School; Nancy Oft Rose, South Eugene High School; David A. Wendt, Keokuk High School; and David Worley, Indiana State University.

Sherwyn P. Morreale, Ph.D.
Associate Director
National Communication Association

INTRODUCTION

The teaching activities contained in this book are designed to help you apply a nationally recognized set of standards for communication education in U. S. public schools. The National Communication Association (NCA) developed and approved 20 *K–12 Standards for Speaking, Listening, and Media Literacy* (see page xiii for a list of these standards). Members of NCA with experience in teaching grades K–12 developed these teaching activities so that all activities maintain the same primary goal: to increase students' communication competence. The activities have been "tested" in communication classrooms and found to be successful in helping students develop speaking, listening, and media literacy competencies. Specifically, these activities are designed to:

- appeal to students of all ability levels
- provide for student interaction and involvement, which is so important to oral communication skills and development
- involve students in sending and receiving messages in a variety of contexts and for a variety of purposes
- provide for integrating oral communication competence instruction across the curriculum

Why Teach Communication?

Competence in oral communication—in speaking, listening, and media literacy—is prerequisite to students' personal and academic success in life. It is probably no surprise to anyone who has attended public schools that teachers deliver most instruction for classroom procedures orally. Consequently, students with ineffective listening skills fail to absorb much of the material to which they are exposed. Their problems increase when they respond incorrectly or inappropriately as a result of poor speaking skills. Students who cannot clearly articulate what they know may be wrongly judged as uneducated or poorly informed. Additionally, speech styles of some students can trigger stereotyped expectations of poor ability, expectations that may become self-fulfilling. At the same time, students who aren't able to effectively ask for help from a teacher will not receive it; typically, such reticent students progress more slowly despite possessing a normal level of aptitude.

Beyond the confines of school, oral communication competence can contribute to students' social adjustment and participation in satisfying interpersonal relationships. Youngsters with poor communication skills are sometimes viewed as unattractive by their peers and have few friendships. Antisocial and violent behavior commonly accompanies underdeveloped social and conflict management skills.

On the positive side, the ability to communicate orally is essential to psychological development. Early research called attention to the fact that self-concept is acquired through interaction with others. In psychological terms, achieving self-actualization usually involves such communication activities as making contributions in groups, exerting influence over others, and being recognized in a socially acceptable manner.

Numerous national surveys and studies highlight the importance of communication competence—and, therefore, communication instruction—to professional success in life (Morreale, Osborn, and Pearson, 2000). According to a U. S. Department of Labor report, communication skills will be in demand across most occupations well into the 21st century (1995). Robert Diamond, who conducts curriculum reform workshops across the country, surveys attendees about how academic curricula should be reformed. Diamond (1997) reports that more than 1,000 representatives of a cross section of disciplines identified communication as one of the top basic competencies for every student graduating from U. S. schools. The *Wall Street Journal* (1998) reported on a survey of 480 companies that found that employers ranked communication abilities first among the desirable personal qualities of future employees. In another survey, 1,000 human resource managers identified oral communication skills as valuable for both obtaining employment and performing successfully on the job (Winsor, Curtis, and Stephens, 1997). Fortune 500 company executives indicated that their future employees need better communication skills, including the ability to work in teams and with people of diverse backgrounds (*Association Trends,* 1997). Finally, case studies conducted in high-wage companies revealed that essential skills for future workers include problem solving, working in groups, and the ability to communicate effectively orally and in writing (Murane and Levy, 1996).

We are living in the information age, in which individuals—students and adults—spend an average of over 3,000 hours with media each year. Media literacy, therefore, is essential to competence and successful living in today's media-saturated world; yet, while most American students are media familiar and media aware, many of them operate at low levels of media literacy. Moreover, although many teachers are incorporating more types of media into their classroom instruction, few teachers have experience helping students increase their skills and knowledge in media literacy and may actually be reinforcing ineffective or inappropriate media practices in the classroom use of media.

Oral communication is fundamental to all other learning. It was in response to this need for communication education and for resources to support it in grades K–12 that NCA developed the set of standards and competencies for students in K–12 for which this publication provides teaching activities. The NCA standards are presented in Figure I.1.

What Are Speaking, Listening, and Media Literacy?

The field of communication focuses on how people use messages to generate meaning within and across various contexts, cultures, channels, and media. The subject matter of communication studies is drawn from both classical traditions and contemporary research. Teachers of communication promote the effective and ethical practice of human communication.

Speaking, listening, and media literacy are three of the elements of communication. Each of these elements has distinguishing characteristics.

- *Speaking:* Speaking is the uniquely human act or process of sharing and exchanging information, ideas, and emotions using oral language. Whether in daily informal interactions or in more formal settings, communicators are required to organize coherent messages, deliver them clearly, and adapt to their listeners.

- *Listening:* Listening is the process of receiving, constructing meaning from, and responding to spoken and/or nonverbal messages. People call on different listening skills depending on whether their goal is to comprehend information, critique and evaluate a message, show empathy for the feelings expressed by others, or appreciate a performance.

- *Media Literacy:* Media literacy is a fundamental competency for literate citizens. A media literate person understands how words, images, and sounds influence the way meanings are created and shared in contemporary society in ways both subtle and profound. A media literate person is equipped to assign value, worth, and meaning to media use and media messages.

How Can This Book Help You Teach Communication?

Traditionally, communication teachers have taught oral communication in one of two ways: (1) an activity approach, in which teachers organize the course objectives and teaching strategies around units of speech activity, such as public speaking, theater, and group communication; or (2) a context approach, in which teachers organize the course objectives and teaching strategies around basic speech communication situations, such as intrapersonal communication, interpersonal communication, and mass communication. The first approach assumes that oral communication skills are best learned in the context of specific activities that emphasize particular skills. The second approach assumes that students acquire communication skills through studying the variety of basic contexts in which communication takes place.

In this text, we offer a third approach to oral communication instruction. This approach emphasizes communication standards and competencies, which cut across oral activities, such as public speaking and discussion, and across communication contexts, such as interpersonal or mass communication. Although the activities in this book may use a particular context or oral communication activity, it is the individual oral communication standard and competency that is paramount. For example, the activity "Block Design" in Unit One uses an interpersonal context, but the competency focuses on understanding the communication process (Standard 1). Figure I.2 lists all of the activities contained in this book and indicates how they link to NCA's 20 standards.

We have included at least two activities for each standard. Each activity includes (1) a description, (2) the objective, (3) procedures for implementing the activity, (4) a debriefing of the activity using follow-up suggestions and/or questions for discussion, and (5) assessment procedures.

References

Diamond, R. (August 1, 1997). "Curriculum Reform Needed If Students Are to Master Core Skills." *Chronicle of Higher Education,* p. B7.

"Graduates Are Not Prepared to Work in Business." (June 1997). *Association Trends,* p. 4.

Murane, R., and Levy, F. (1996). *Teaching the New Basic Skills.* New York: Free Press.

Morreale, S., Osborn, M., and Pearson, J. (2000). "Why Communication Is Important: A Rationale for the Centrality of the Discipline." *Journal for the Association of Communication Administration* 29, pp. 1–25.

U. S. Department of Labor. (1995). "Career Projections to 2005." *Fastest Growing Careers.* Chevy Chase, MD: National Certification Commission.

Winsor, J., Curtis, D., and Stephens, R. (1997). "National Preferences in Business and Communication Education: A Survey Update." *Journal for the Association of Communication Administration* 3, pp. 170–179.

"Work Week." (December 29, 1998). *Wall Street Journal,* p. A1.

FIGURE I.1	*NCA's Standards for Speaking, Listening, and Media Literacy in K–12 Education.*

FUNDAMENTALS OF EFFECTIVE COMMUNICATION

Competent communicators demonstrate knowledge and understanding of . . .

1. the relationships among the components of the communication process (speaker, listener, message, medium, feedback, and noise).

2. the influence of the individual, relationship, and situation on communication.

3. the role of communication in the development and maintenance of personal relationships.

4. the role of communication in creating meaning, influencing thought, and making decisions.

Competent communicators demonstrate the ability to . . .

5. demonstrate sensitivity to diversity when communicating.

6. enhance relationships and resolve conflict using appropriate and effective communication strategies.

7. evaluate communication styles, strategies, and content based on their aesthetic and functional worth.

8. show sensitivity to the ethical issues associated with communication in a democratic society.

SPEAKING

Competent speakers demonstrate . . .

9. knowledge and understanding of the speaking process.

10. the ability to adapt communication strategies appropriately and effectively according to the needs of the situation and setting.

11. the ability to use language that clarifies, persuades, and/or inspires while respecting differences in listeners' backgrounds.

12. the ability to manage or overcome communication anxiety.

LISTENING

Competent listeners demonstrate . . .

13. knowledge and understanding of the listening process.

14. the ability to use appropriate and effective listening skills for a given communication situation and setting.

15. the ability to identify and manage barriers to listening.

MEDIA LITERACY

Media-literate communicators demonstrate . . .

16. knowledge and understanding of the ways people use media in their personal and public lives.

17. knowledge and understanding of the complex relationships among audiences and media content.

18. knowledge and understanding that media content is produced within social and cultural contexts.

19. knowledge and understanding of the commercial nature of media.

20. the ability to use media to communicate to specific audiences.

FIGURE 1.2	*Activities for fundamentals of effective communication, speaking, listening, and media literacy.*

Appropriate grade levels are noted in parentheses.

FUNDAMENTALS OF EFFECTIVE COMMUNICATION (UNIT ONE)

Standard 1

1.1 Block Design (7–8)

1.2 Name That Analogy: The Communication Game (9–10)

1.3 Character Communication (9–10, 11–12)

Standard 2

1.4 Social Customs (9–10)

1.5 Characters in Conflict (9–10, 11–12)

Standard 3

1.6 Introducing Me! (7–8)

1.7 Evolving Perceptions (9–10, 11–12)

1.8 What's Appropriate? (11–12)

Standard 4

1.9 The Meaning Exercise (9–10)

1.10 Poetry in Motion (9–10, 11–12)

Standard 5

1.11 Intercultural Interview (7–8, 9–10)

1.12 Becoming a Family (9–10)

Standard 6

1.13 Talking to Parents (7–8, 9–10)

1.14 Why Don't You Understand Me? (9–10, 11–12)

Standard 7

1.15 It Just Sounds Pretty (7–8)

1.16 Haiku (7–8, 9–10)

1.17 And the *Other* Moral of the Story Is . . . (9–10, 11–12)

Standard 8

1.18 Don't Judge Me by My Cover (7–8, 9–10)

1.19 What's Your View? (9–10, 11–12)

SPEAKING (UNIT TWO)

Standard 9

2.1 Delivery Cards (7–8, 9–10)

2.2 Look Who's Listening: The Importance of Subaudiences in Public Speaking (7–8, 9–10)

2.3 Pointers for Polished Public Speaking (9–10, 11–12)

2.4 Who Is the Listener? (9–10, 11–12)

Standard 10

2.5 Tell and Show; Listen and Draw (7–8)

2.6 My Mind's Made Up; Don't Confuse Me with the Facts (9–10, 11–12)

2.7 Using the Internet as an Information Source (10–12)

Standard 11

2.8 Transitional Stories (9–10)

2.9 Word Power (9–10, 11–12)

Standard 12

2.10 Using Group Speaking to Overcome Anxiety (7–8)

2.11 Choral Oral Literacy (7–8, 9–10)

2.12 Reducing Speaking Anxiety Through Speech Preparation (9–10, 11–12)

2.13 Public Speaking: Reducing Anxiety and Revealing a Process (9–10, 11–12)

LISTENING (UNIT THREE)

Standard 13

3.1 Let's Tell a Story (7–8, 9–10)

3.2 Invisible Speeches (11–12)

Standard 14

3.3 The Listening Box (7–8, 9–10)

3.4 What I Hear You Saying Is . . . (7–8, 9–10)

3.5 To Tell the Truth (11–12)

Standard 15

3.6 Talking Stick (9–10)

3.7 May I Quote You? (11–12)

MEDIA LITERACY (UNIT FOUR)

Standard 16

4.1 My Daily Media (9–10, 11–12)

4.2 Defining Media Channels (9–10, 11–12)

Standard 17

4.3 Media Characters and Real People (7–8)

4.4 Millions of Magazines (9–10)

4.5 Target Audience (11–12)

Standard 18

4.6 A Peak Behind the Scenes (7–8)

4.7 As Time Goes By (9–10, 11–12)

4.8 Rock-n-Listen (9–10, 11–12)

Standard 19

4.9 Advertising's Appeal (7–8)

4.10 Look at Me—I'm Better and Faster! (9–10)

4.11 Cross Marketing and the Big Five (11–12)

Standard 20

4.12 The Medium and the Message (7–8, 9–10)

4.13 In the News (9–10, 11–12)

4.14 I'm Your Candidate! (11–12)

FUNDAMENTALS OF EFFECTIVE COMMUNICATION

Introduction

All of us have been communicating all our lives. This communicating often is something to which we give little thought. In fact, because we have been communicating all our lives, we think we know how to do it well. However, we all can think of times in which our communication has been less than effective. We are not always understood, nor do we always understand others. This is because communication is a complex process—one that is dynamic, continually occurring, continually changing. Communication does not end when we leave our communication partner but continues as each partner thinks about the communication that has occurred. Have you ever thought, "Oh, I wish I had said (or done) . . ."? If so, then our point is made!

Defining Communication

Communication is not easy to define. In 1970, a communication scholar reviewed academic articles and textbooks and identified 95 definitions of human communication (Dance, 1970). No doubt this number has increased since 1970. Why so many definitions? The reason is that communication is a complex process. It is beyond the scope of this book to discuss the theoretical issues inherent in defining communication (for more in-depth information, please see the resources included in Unit Five), but for our purposes, we can define human communication as *shared meaning between two or more people using a symbol system.*

Components of the Communication Process

To communicate, we need people (all with their own sets of beliefs and values, their own perceptions of the world, their own cultural heritage, and so forth), a message (verbal and nonverbal—both are symbol systems), and a channel through which the message flows (for example, written memos, face-to-face interaction, electronic mail, television, print media). Often there is noise in the channel. Noise is any signal that disrupts the accuracy of the message being sent. Noise may be physical (someone tapping a pencil on a desk, a room that is too hot, chalk scraping on a chalkboard) or psychological (daydreaming, personal problems, attitudes). These distractions can cause inaccuracy in communication—preventing the message sent from being the message received. Finally, communication involves feedback. We do not talk just to a wall; rather, we talk to people who send a message back to us indicating how the message we sent is being received. Therefore, the communication process includes six components (speaker, listener, message, medium, feedback, and noise) and can be modeled as shown in Figure 1.1.

FIGURE 1.1	*A model of communication.*

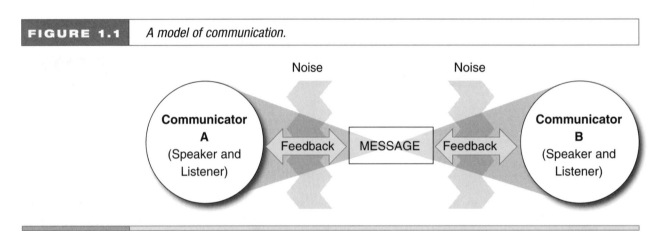

Characteristics of Communication

Communication is a transactional process that is complex and symbolic and has both a content and a relational component. When we say that communication is a *transactional* process, we mean that each person in the communication is simultaneously both a source and a receiver. In other words, as I send you a message, I am also receiving a message from you in the form of nonverbal communication (a frown, a smile, a quizzical look, body posture). Similarly, as you send me those messages, you are receiving my messages (see a transactional model in Figure 1.1). An axiom of communication is that you cannot *not* communicate. Whenever we are perceived by another, we communicate—if only through our nonverbal communication.

The process notion of communication suggests that communication is continuous, unrepeatable, and irreversible. As mentioned above, communication continues even after communicators part. We think about what we said and did. We think about what we will say and do the next time we meet. What was said and done in each meeting affects what is said and done in our next meeting. Communication is an irreversible process—we cannot unsay or undo something. We can say that we are sorry, but that does not change the fact that we said something or did something that hurt the other person. Similarly, communication is unrepeatable. One philosopher suggests that you cannot step in the same river twice. The river has continued to flow, and you are not the same person with every minute that passes.

Communication is complex. It has been said that when two people communicate, there are actually six people communicating. Because communication begins with the self, each person communicating has a view of herself. This affects what she decides to communicate. In addition, each person has a view of the other person; this also affects what each decides to communicate. And finally, each has a view of what the other person thinks of her, and this affects what each decides to communicate. On top of all this, communication takes place within a context—where the communication is taking place, what time of day it is, what the topic is, and so forth all affect communication choices.

Communication is symbolic. One communication axiom is that meanings are in people, not in words. Our words, gestures, and facial expressions are symbols—not the actual things. For example, the word "chair" is a symbol. It is not the actual chair. My idea of chair might be a big, overstuffed chair. Your idea might be a straight-backed, wooden desk chair. Our meanings are in our minds, not in the word. A smile might mean happiness to me but be a way to mask anger to you. Thus, communication is symbolic.

Finally, communication has both a content and a relationship component. Whenever we communicate, we do so on these two levels. To understand these levels, consider the following example. A student comes to your office to discuss a problem she is having with an assignment. She knocks on your slightly opened door and says, "Can I talk to you for a minute?" As you continue grading the papers in front of you, not looking at the student, you say, "Yes, come in." Your content message indicates a specific behavior the student should perform—she should enter your office. However, your relationship message states quite clearly that you do not wish to be disturbed. The relationship message can indicate how you view the other person, how you view yourself, and how you view the relationship between you and the other person.

Standards of Communication

The eight standards in this category prepare students for communicating effectively in a variety of ways in diverse situations. The first four standards are *knowledge-based* standards. They include

1. understanding the components of the communication process and their relationship to one another,

2. understanding the influence of individuals, relationships, and situations on communication,

3. understanding the role of communication in developing and maintaining personal relationships, and

4. understanding how communication helps us create meaning, influences our thoughts, and helps us make decisions.

The second four standards deal with communication *skills*. These standards provide opportunities for students to demonstrate the ability to

5. show sensitivity to diversity when communicating,

6. enhance relationships and resolve conflict using appropriate and effective communication strategies,

7. evaluate communication styles, strategies, and content, and

8. show sensitivity to ethical issues.

The activities in this section were selected because they provide students with opportunities to learn about the communication process and apply that knowledge in specific situations.

ACTIVITY

1.1 Block Design

Standard 1: Competent communicators demonstrate knowledge and understanding of the relationships among the components of the communication process (speaker, listener, message, medium, feedback, and noise).

Grade Levels: 7–8

Description: This activity requires pairs of students to give and listen to directions in front of their classmates. Students will become aware of the components of the communication process and realize the value of asking questions for clarification and providing feedback.

Objective: Students will verify the listener's understanding of their answers and understand the importance of checking for comprehension.

Materials: Two sets of 10 blocks of various shapes, textures, and sizes

Procedure:
1. Seat two students back-to-back in the front of the classroom. In front of each student put identical piles of 10 blocks of various shapes, textures, and sizes.
2. Ask Student A to make a design with the blocks.
3. Have Student A tell Student B how to assemble the blocks into an identical pattern. Neither may turn around to look at the other's blocks, but students may ask questions.
4. Tape-record the dialogue.
5. After Students A and B are satisfied that their blocks are arranged in identical patterns, they should stop and compare them.

Debriefing: Play the recording of the interaction. Listen for questions and the answers to them. The following questions might be considered during discussion:

1. Were the questions clear and sufficient in number?
2. Did the student answering verify that the other student had understood?
3. What could she have asked to make certain the answer had been understood? For example, did Student A give an answer and then ask a comprehension-checking question (as in the dialogue below)?

   A : Place the round block on the smallest square block.
   B : Which round block?
   A : The round block that is smooth. Do you know which one I mean?
   B : Yes, not the round block that has rough edges.
   A : Yes, the smooth one.

4. Were there places where checking on the receiver's comprehension would have prevented errors? What additional questions would help?

   Relate the answers to the components of the communication process. For example:

1. What types of noise were present?

2. What would have happened if the message had been relayed through written rather than spoken means?

3. What forms of feedback did you hear?

Repeat the experiment with two new students. Instruct Student A to check on Student B's comprehension after answering each question. Compare the accuracy of the design and the amount of time taken in each instance.

Assessment: You may assess the students' use of questions by comparing the accuracy of the two block designs. The second set of students, who will check comprehension after answering questions, should produce designs that are more similar than did the first set. You can check on the learning of all students by having students write a set of directions and repeat the activity with a partner. Have them include comprehension-checking questions with their directions. After they finish the oral direction giving, have them report on their success and suggest some questions they could have asked that would have made the results even more successful.

1.2	**Name That Analogy:** The Communication Game

Standard 1:   Competent communicators demonstrate knowledge and understanding of the relationships among the components of the communication process (speaker, listener, message, medium, feedback, and noise).

Grade Levels: 9–10

Description: This activity asks groups of students to create a simile that they develop to help describe the communication process. By developing comparisons to something familiar and then sharing them with the class, students come to better understand that communication is not just one person speaking and another absorbing but, rather, is an active and complex process.

Objective: Students will learn about the relationship among the components of the communication process and gain an understanding of communication as an active and dynamic process.

Materials: None

Procedure: 1. Put students into small groups and ask them to complete the following statement:

"Communication is like a game of ___ because ___."

The analogy can be made to a board game, a computer game, a card game, or a type of sport, as long as the group can justify its choice.

2. After students select a game, have them list as many ways in which communication is like their game as they can generate. For example, "Communication is like swimming because . . ." What follows might be statements such as "It sometimes takes courage to jump in and do it"; "Sometimes it's really important to keep your mouth shut"; or "Taking lessons can make you a lot better at it."

3. After students have listed several points of comparison, ask each group to explain and justify their communication game analogy.

4. As the analogies are presented, discuss the characteristics associated with each.

Debriefing: Use these comparisons to discuss the communication components (see Figure 1.1) and the elements involved in the communication process. Compare and contrast the various analogies to help students understand that communication is a complex, dynamic, active process.

Assessment: Ask students individually to create and explain an original analogy using something other than a game. Note whether they can use their analogy to explain how communication is an active process and how the components of the process either work together to produce successful communication or sometimes result in problems that work against success.

ACTIVITY

1.3   Character Communication

Standard 1: Competent communicators demonstrate knowledge and understanding of the relationships among the components of the communications process (speaker, listener, message, medium, feedback, and noise).

Grade Levels: 9–10, 11–12

Description: In small groups, students use the dialogue in short stories to discover and understand the components of the communication process.

Objective: Students will understand the components of the communication process and apply them to their reading of literature.

Materials: A short story, pen, and paper

Procedure:
1. Use Figure 1.1 (page 2) to lead a discussion on the components of the communication process (speaker, listener, message, medium, feedback, and noise). Help students understand the role each component plays in communication.

2. Assign the class to read a short story that contains dialogue.

3. Ask students, in small groups, to examine a segment of dialogue, looking for examples of each of the components. Students should pay close attention to the descriptions of the characters' behaviors as well as to the words, thus exploring both verbal and nonverbal communication. For example:

    Dialogue segment:

    Young boy: Mom, where are you going? Why do you have to go? When will you be home? I don't want to stay with Aunt Belle.

    Mother: Don't make such a fuss. I won't be gone long. Just be a good boy.

    (Mother turns and walks out of the room).

4. Begin discussion by asking the following questions:
    a. Who is the speaker? Who is the listener? (Point out that in this case, as with most conversations, both characters are playing both parts.)

    b. What is the boy's message? What is the content of his message? What are the emotions behind it?

    c. Does the mother appear to understand the comment? The emotions? What feedback does she give?

    d. What information in the story about the boy and his mother helps the reader understand the dialogue and its meaning?

    e. Is there any noise, such as troubling emotions, in this segment? If so, what is it? What effect does it have?

    f. Based on this piece of communication, what do you predict will happen next?

Debriefing: Lead a discussion on how an author must use all components of the communication process to create readable prose. All of the elements must be believable for readers to find the characters and their words and actions authentic. Students should report what components they found. Discuss any disagreements the groups may have.

Assessment: Test students on their knowledge of the components of the communication process. Provide a segment of dialogue from a class reading, and ask the students to analyze it in light of the aspects of communication. Students could also write their own short dialogue and explain how it demonstrates all of the components of the communication process.

ACTIVITY

1.4   Social Customs

Standard 2: Competent communicators demonstrate knowledge and understanding of the influence of the individual, relationship, and situation on communication.

Grade Levels: 9–10

Description: This activity gives students experience with role-plays designed to prompt awareness and discussion of social rituals in adolescent lives. This discussion should alert students to the importance of these rituals and to standards for acceptable communication patterns for use in the rituals.

Objective: By performing and analyzing social rituals necessary for functioning as a teenager in society, students will understand how context influences communication.

Materials: Role-play situations (see below)

Procedure: Ask selected students to perform the following role-plays while other class members observe.

1. Two friends who used to be neighbors and best friends in elementary school meet. One friend moved to another city in junior high and is in town visiting relatives. The two meet in one of the following places: a restaurant (one is just arriving and is waiting for a table; the other is leaving), a department store, or the concession stand at a movie theater a few minutes before the movie is to begin.

2. A teacher, parents, and a student gather in the teacher's office for an annual parent–student–teacher conference. The teacher is responsible for leading the meeting.

3. A boy arrives at the home of a girl he is dating for the first time. The girl's father answers the door and lets the boy in. The boy must wait a few minutes until the girl arrives. The girl's older brother is also home.

Debriefing: Discuss the approaches students took in each situation. Ask such questions as:

1. Were the approaches appropriate?

2. What did the communicators do and say that was appropriate? Inappropriate?

3. How do you know when a communication behavior is appropriate? List such qualities as:

   - is clearly understood,
   - does not needlessly offend,
   - makes a favorable impression,
   - takes into account the people involved,
   - the setting and the relationships of the people

4. What effect did these communication choices have on what happened?

5. What experiences have you had in similar situations? How did you deal with each situation?

6. What would you do differently if given another opportunity?

Assessment: Ask students to observe family members, teachers, friends, and characters on television and in movies for a week to determine whether there are social rituals that are "standard" in our culture. Have students list rituals they found and explain their importance to our culture. This can be done orally or in written form.

Show a taped segment of a communication interaction and ask students:

1. How did the speakers take into account their audience? How successfully?

2. How did speakers take into account the setting? How successfully?

3. How did the speakers take into account their relationship to the listener(s)? How successfully?

4. What could the speakers have done to be more effective?

ACTIVITY

1.5   Characters in Conflict

Standard 2:   Competent communicators demonstrate knowledge and understanding of the influence of the individual, relationship, and situation on communication.

Grade Levels: 9–10, 11–12

Description: By using examples from literature, this activity helps students evaluate how relationships are maintained and conflicts are resolved.

Objective: Students will understand the importance of the individual and the choices individuals make in maintaining relationships and resolving conflicts.

Materials: Scenes of conflict and friendship from literature, pen, and paper

Procedure: 1. Discuss with students the nature and frequency of conflict. One useful way to think of conflict is as a disagreement involving a difference in goals—for example, a parent has a priority goal of child safety and a child has a goal of independence.

2. Select a passage from a piece of literature in which the characters are in conflict and are working to build or maintain relationships (possibilities include *Of Mice and Men, Romeo and Juliet, A Tale of Two Cities, The Scarlet Letter, The Pearl, The Bean Trees*).

3. After they have read the passage, have students discuss the causes of the conflicts, the importance of individual choices in maintaining relationships, and what strategies the characters are using or not using to make the situation better.

4. Have students role-play the scene from the passage with alternative choices of behavior—some with positive results and some with negative results.

Debriefing: Lead a discussion on the choices each character made in the passage. As a class, decide what strategies were effective and which were ineffective. Discuss the students' choices in their role-playing, and work together to discover how the story would change if the characters were to make the same choices as the students.

Assessment: Evaluate the choices and role-playing the students created. Have students write about a situation in which they were in conflict with someone. What strategies did they use? What would they have done differently? What can they do now if the conflict is still happening? Look for insight into the nature of conflict and knowledge of conflict management strategies.

ACTIVITY

1.6 | Introducing Me!

Standard 3: Competent communicators demonstrate knowledge and understanding of the role of communication in the development and maintenance of personal relationships.

Grade Levels: 7–8

Description: This whole-class activity encourages students to think about their choices in introducing themselves and others in various situations. Students role-play and then discuss situations with the class. This activity helps students recognize social rituals as a form of communication that helps develop relationships.

Objective: Students will perform social rituals necessary for their age and ability level, thereby demonstrating knowledge of the role of communication in developing relationships.

Materials: None

Procedure: Ask students to role-play introducing themselves and/or another person. Situations include:

1. You are a new student at school and know only a few people. You are looking for a place to sit in the cafeteria, and the only empty places are by people you do not know. Sit down next to them, introduce yourself, and make small talk.

2. You are with your mother in the grocery store and see your math teacher, who is the meanest teacher you have. She says hello to you first and stops in the aisle. Introduce her to your mother.

3. Your school is involved in a money-making project, selling candy door-to-door. Your next-door neighbors are new. Introduce yourself, and explain your purpose.

Select two or three sets of students for each role-playing situation. While those students are preparing their role-plays, discuss with the class when introductions are used and why they are important.

Debriefing: Ask the following questions during the discussion:

1. Were there any differences in the approaches taken by separate groups for the same role-play?

2. Could one approach be considered better or more acceptable than another?

3. What are the standard procedures one should go through in introducing oneself to another person?

4. How should one refer to parents when introducing them (Mr., Mrs., complete names)?

5. What embarrassing situations have you experienced in being introduced or in introducing someone?

6. Could these situations have been prevented? How?

7. How might the way the individuals were introduced affect the relationship between the participants?

Assessment: Give students one or two additional situations that involve introductions, and have them prepare explanations of acceptable procedures and sample dialogue for the situation.

ACTIVITY

1.7   Evolving Perceptions

Standard 3: Competent communicators demonstrate knowledge and understanding of the role of communication in the development and maintenance of personal relationships.

Grade Levels: 9–10, 11–12

Description: This activity uses literature to explore the nature of perceptions in relationships. By thinking about how a character views the world, students gain insight into how that view affects the communication between characters in a relationship.

Objective: Students will realize that another's viewpoint is usually more complex than it initially appears.

Materials: None

Procedure:
1. Ask each student to write one or two paragraphs about a character in a film or novel. This should be a character whose words and actions seem very clear at first but who, as the story progresses, says or does something unexpected—revealing deeper, more complicated intentions. Students should choose a character they thought they easily understood at first but who surprised them later. (Possible characters include Emily in *Our Town,* Captain Keller in *The Miracle Worker,* Hamlet, Creon in *Antigone,* George in *Of Mice and Men,* Brutus in *Julius Caesar,* the jurors in *Twelve Angry Men,* and all of the characters in *Lord of the Flies.*)
2. After students have written a description of their first impression of the character and the later change in that impression, ask volunteers to describe their examples and explain what actions and/or dialogue led to the impressions.

Debriefing: Use the following questions to facilitate discussion:
1. If a person has a deeply held opinion, it is usually caused by some personal experience in that person's background. Do we need to have had the same experience in order to understand the person's view?
2. When you express an opinion or viewpoint, are there usually additional thoughts in your mind that are left unsaid?
3. What implication does that have for talking to others about their opinions?
4. How do the perceptions we have of others affect our relationships with them?

Assessment: The papers written during this activity should show students' ability to understand how their own first impressions may change as they gain more information about a person. Discussion should result in students understanding that when they talk to others, past experiences have influenced their opinions and that they can come to better understand and relate to others by knowing more about how their views were formed.

ACTIVITY

1.8   What's Appropriate

Standard 3:   Competent communicators demonstrate knowledge and understanding of the role of communication in the development and maintenance of personal relationships.

Grade Levels: 11–12

Description: This activity uses a job interview setting to help students see how the setting and purpose of communication influence what is considered appropriate with regard to the various communication elements, such as topic choice, language, use of voice, and body language.

Objective: Students will increase verbal and nonverbal skills in a variety of social situations.

Materials: Job descriptions

Procedure: 1. Arrange the room so that several chairs represent a waiting room, with a desk for a receptionist near the group of chairs. Design another part of the room as an office, with a desk and an additional chair placed in front of the desk.

2. Select three or four students to serve as interviewees; one student should serve as a receptionist and one as the interviewer. Brief descriptions of a real or hypothetical job should be supplied to the interviewer and interviewees. Students can write these ahead of time as a writing assignment, or the descriptions can be taken from current local want ads. Read or display the ads on the overhead before the role-playing begins.

3. Each interviewee should enter the waiting area, make initial inquiries with the receptionist, and then take a seat. The interviewees should spend time as a group, making small talk with strangers while waiting to be called for an interview.

4. Once a student is called in for an interview, the interviewer and interviewee should role-play the initial few minutes of a job interview that include introductions and background information.

5. If students are new to the interviewing process, review some of the typical opening questions used, such as those seeking background information on previous jobs held and education and those used to screen candidates, such as, "Why do you want this job?" and "What are your strengths and weaknesses?" Additional hypothetical jobs can be supplied and other students chosen to role-play. Other class members should serve as observers during the process.

Debriefing: Discuss the role-plays with the class by asking:

1. What verbal and nonverbal behaviors did you observe in each of the three situations? Were there any differences in formality, language, or information shared?

2. What is "appropriate" behavior in each of the three situations? Did each of the subjects exhibit appropriate behavior?

3. Describe your own experience performing social rituals in the workplace or as a customer.

4. What inappropriate behaviors have you used or observed? What made them so? What were the consequences of using them?

Assessment: One week after the activity, ask students to write a brief description of an employment-related incident (either as an employee or as a customer) that they experienced or observed since the role-playing and which required using social rituals. Ask them to assess their skills and/or those of others in the situation. Or, play a videotape of a job interview and/or a small talk scenario and have the class answer questions about it similar to those used in the class discussion.

ACTIVITY

1.9   The Meaning Exercise

Standard 4:   Competent communicators demonstrate knowledge and understanding of the role of communication in creating meaning, influencing thought, and making decisions.

Grade Levels: 7–8, 9–10

Description: By exploring the denotative and connotative meanings of common words, students begin to understand the importance and power of language.

Objective: Students will be made aware of the power of language and words and how different communication choices can affect meaning and can influence our thoughts.

Materials: Pen, paper

Procedure:
1. Break the class into small groups.

2. Give each group a list of words such as the following, adding those currently in use by your class: *good, terrible, funny, strange, happy,* and so forth.

3. Ask each group to create dialogues in which the meanings of the words change according to the situations and contexts in which they are used.

4. Have students role-play for the class how the meanings of words can change, by acting out their dialogues. Begin with simple dialogues that focus on using a word differently.

   Sample dialogue—Version 1

   A: I'm trying to save energy.
   B. So how are you doing that?
   A. I'm going to hang out all my wash and let it air dry.

   Sample dialogue—Version 2

   A. Where is José?
   B. Oh, I bet he's in the computer lab. That's where he likes to hang out.

5. Have students move on to writing more sophisticated scripts that use words in more subtle ways, with the focus on the connotation of the words rather than denotation.

Debriefing: Lead a discussion on how words have both denotative and connotative meanings. Also discuss how culture and individual experience create meaning for words. Possible questions include:

1. Why is it easier to understand your friends than your parents' friends?

2. What are some words you use that your parents don't understand?

3. What happens when you use these words when talking to your parents?

4. What are some new words to express emotions that are being used by students today that were not used by students five years ago?

5. Are there words common to your culture that other cultures would not understand, even when translated into English?

Assessment: Students should be able to talk or write about the differences between denotation and connotation. Students could be evaluated on their understanding of how culture and experience create different meaning for different words. This understanding should be reflected in the word choices students make when speaking and writing.

1.10 Poetry in Motion

Standard 4: Competent communicators demonstrate knowledge and understanding of the role of communication in creating meaning, influencing thought, and making decisions.

Grade Levels: 9–10, 11–12

Description: This activity uses poetry to help students explore the emotional meanings of a message.

Objective: Students will recognize the power of words and the emotional meanings of a message and understand how different communication choices can influence thoughts.

Materials: A variety of free-style and verse poetry, including haikus

Procedure:
1. Students may select poetry of their own, or you may select poetry for the class. Many examples are available in printed collections of haiku or on the Internet at such sites as www.teenwriting.about.com or www.geocities.com/Tokyo/Island/5022/, where the works of Basho are discussed.

2. After students individually select a poem to analyze, ask them to underline the words they find to have the strongest emotional attachment for them.

3. Using a thesaurus or their own knowledge, students should replace those words with synonyms. For example, consider the following haiku written by Naro, a 17-year-old from Turkey:

   I need a nice home

   With my sweet cute yellow dog

   Oh what a nice hope!

   Depending on their experiences, students might underline the word "dog" (perhaps if they have one) or "home" (if it reminds them of theirs). The words could change to make the poem read differently, such as:

   I want a bland house

   With my sugary perky maize canine

   Oh what a pleasant desire!

   Not only is the meaning affected, but the emotional power also is lost.

4. In small groups, have students read the poems aloud with both word choices. Students should also try reading the poems with different emotions and emphasis.

5. Students could also write their own haikus and then have someone else rewrite them with synonyms.

Debriefing: Lead a discussion on how the poems change with the new words. Possible questions include:

1. Does the poem have more or less emotional meaning?

2. Why do some words have strong emotional meanings to some and not to others?

3. How does the meaning change when the poems are read with more emotion or emphasis?

Assessment: Students should be able to talk or write about their reactions to the poems and to the word choices they made. Students' haikus could be evaluated on the choices they made and their readings of the poems.

ACTIVITY

1.11   Intercultural Interview

Standard 5:   Competent communicators demonstrate the ability to demonstrate sensitivity to diversity when communicating.

Grade Levels: 7–8, 9–10

Description: In this activity, students interview individuals from another culture, helping them to understand the role of culture in communication.

Objective: Students will communicate more effectively with a person from another culture by gaining a better understanding of that person's culture.

Materials: "Intercultural Interview" worksheet

Procedure: 1. Review with students a definition of culture such as that offered by Dictionary.com:

   "The totality of socially transmitted behavior patterns, arts, beliefs, institutions, and all other products of human work and thought."

   2. Discuss with students the culture that serves as the setting for a piece of literature the class is reading, or use this assignment to help students understand a piece of literature they are reading independently.

   3. Hand out the "Intercultural Interview" worksheet to students. Instruct students to follow its directions.

Debriefing: Have students give a brief oral report or write a paper describing what they learned. If several students did a similar culture, they could give a panel presentation to the class. Be sure that students understand that each culture is, by definition, different and that different is not bad—just different. Help students see the impact that one's culture has on lifestyles and beliefs. Ask students how what they learned will help them talk and listen to someone from that culture in the future.

Assessment: Students should demonstrate in their reports and discussion that they have come to understand a little about how others live and show that they have developed a respect for other cultures. They should be able to translate that understanding into behaviors that result in more effective communication with people from other backgrounds.

Intercultural Interview

Interview someone from a culture different than your own. It can be someone from another country, a different-size city or part of your country, a different religion, a different age-group, or a different type of family. After you select—but before you interview—the person, research his or her culture. You can do any or all of the following:

- Read an article from an encyclopedia on the person's culture, religion, country, and so forth.

- Do a search on the Internet using the person's culture as a search term.

- Talk to another member of that culture and ask for a description of important characteristics.

After learning about the culture, write a list of conclusions you drew and questions you would like to ask. When you conduct the interview, take notes on the answers to your questions and check to see whether your conclusions were correct. Find out as much as you can about how life in that person's culture is similar to and different from your own.

Possible questions:

_____

_____

_____

_____

_____

_____

_____

_____

_____

_____

_____

_____

_____

1.12   Becoming a Family

Standard 5: Competent communicators demonstrate the ability to demonstrate sensitivity to diversity when communicating.

Grade Levels: 9–10

Description: This activity uses a role-play to help students explore the influence that different roles and age have in forming a speaker's perspective.

Objective: Students will describe the opinions of others without prejudice.

Materials: Copies of the "Ruth's Story" scenario

Procedure:
1. Divide the class into groups of roughly equal size:

   Group A—all male

   Group B—all female

   Groups C and D—mixed male and female

2. Have each group read the scenario.
   - Groups A and C should decide how they think Joe would describe a good daughter.
   - Groups B and D should decide how they think Ruth would describe a good daughter.

   Each person in each group should contribute at least one suggestion toward the complete description of the character's opinion.

3. After five minutes, have a spokesperson from each group go to the front of the room and inform the class of the group's description. Groups may not make any changes in their lists of points or descriptions after the reports have begun.

4. List points on the board as given.

5. Ask Groups A and C each to send a "Joe" and Groups B and D each to send a "Ruth" to form two dyads. Each dyad completes the following steps in front of the class:

   a. Joe summarizes his opinion of a good daughter.

   b. Ruth restates Joe's opinion to his satisfaction.

   c. Ruth summarizes her opinion of a good daughter.

   d. Joe restates Ruth's opinion to her satisfaction.

Debriefing: The following questions might be considered during the discussion:
1. Do you see any differences of opinion about what makes a good daughter?
2. Why do you think that these differences exist?
3. Do you think Ruth and Joe needed to find out each other's opinion?
4. Can you summarize Joe and Ruth's opinions without contributing negative connotations through your choice of language, tone of voice, gestures, or facial expression?

Assessment: Upon request, individual students should be able to restate either character's position fairly and to the satisfaction of the teacher and the class. Replicate the activity with a new scenario. Ask each student to create and explain the descriptions, pointing out factors that would result in two different positions.

Scenario: Ruth's Story

Ruth has lived with her mother, Mary, since her parents divorced several years ago. Mary has always worked, and Ruth has learned to accept responsibility for her own behavior and to assume her share of the household duties. Recently, Mary married Joe, a fine, hardworking man from a large second-generation American family. Ruth and Joe always got along well before the marriage. Since the marriage, however, their relationship has deteriorated. Since Mary works afternoons and early evenings, Ruth's job is to prepare dinner for herself and Joe. When she goes out with her boyfriend, she sometimes leaves before Joe has finished eating, so she cleans up the table and the kitchen after she comes home. She is almost always home before midnight because she doesn't want her mother to stay awake worrying about her.

Ruth has noticed that Joe seems angry and tight-lipped when she leaves. Last night, she heard Mary and Joe arguing after she got home and she heard her name mentioned. This morning at breakfast, Ruth could tell that her mother had been crying. When she asked what was the matter, Mary said that Joe said that she was a bad mother and that Ruth was growing up "trashy." Ruth knows that Mary is usually very happy with Joe, and she is anxious for their marriage to last. When she asks Joe why he is giving her mother a hard time about her, Joe says that Mary should be ashamed of herself for letting Ruth neglect her duties and stay out all hours.

In Ruth's opinion, Mary is a good mother and she is a good daughter. She does not understand why Joe's opinion differs, but she is anxious not to cause further trouble between her mother and stepfather. She asks Joe if they cannot share their opinions about how she should act to meet his approval and at the same time allow her the self-determination to which she is accustomed.

A C T I V I T Y

1.13 Talking to Parents

Standard 6: Competent communicators demonstrate the ability to enhance relationships and resolve conflict using appropriate and effective communication strategies.

Grade Levels: 7–8, 9–10

Description: This activity provides an opportunity to practice dealing with conflict situations that come from students' own concerns and experiences.

Objective: Students will generate options for managing conflict in parent–teen communication.

Materials: One index card for each student

Procedure:
1. Ask students to write down on an index card a problem or difficulty they have experienced (or witnessed) related to a parent–child relationship—for example, disagreements concerning curfew, appropriate dress, future plans, or responsibilities at home. No names should be used.

2. Collect these cards at random and put them in a box.

3. Ask for a student volunteer to come to the front of the class. The student picks out one of the cards at random and reads it aloud. The student then talks as if faced with the problem or difficulty on the card and suggests how he might deal with it. Encourage other class members to add other suggestions. Direct the class toward listing alternative ways of dealing with the issue. Students also could be enlisted to role-play the scene.

4. After some resolution is reached on the issue, have students summarize the main ideas generated for dealing with the problem.

5. Ask for another student volunteer to select a new card. This continues as long as time and interest allow.

6. Another way to work with the role-playing is to have students call out "freeze" during the role-play. The actors should freeze, and the student who called out should go on stage to replace one of the actors. This gives the viewers another perception of how the scene might be played.

Debriefing: Use the following questions for discussion:
1. How would we select the best idea of the ones offered?
2. What specific communication skills would be useful in this situation?
3. How would these skills be used in the situation?
4. How could you tell if the situations were resolved?

Assessment: Students should be able to produce solutions that reflect empathy and good problem-solving skills. They should be able to offer multiple solutions to a conflict situation and evaluate the possibilities as to effectiveness. They should demonstrate in their own communication behaviors a better ability to resolve conflicts.

ACTIVITY

1.14   Why Don't You Understand Me?

Standard 6: Competent communicators demonstrate the ability to enhance relationships and resolve conflict using appropriate and effective communication strategies.

Grade Levels: 9–10, 11–12

Description: This activity places students in groups to discuss and evaluate their own and others' messages. By evaluating the communication process and focusing on how communication behaviors enhance relationships or create conflicts, students analyze and apply previously covered concepts of effective communication to their own lives.

Objective: Students will evaluate oral messages and recognize what signals indicate misunderstanding of a message.

Materials: Self-Evaluation Form

Procedure:
1. Divide students into small groups of five to seven members.
2. Give each group a separate topic from the list below (or create topics of your own based on student interests or current events in your school, city, state, region, or even the nation). Possible topics include:
   - Should the interstate highway speed be raised? Or lowered?
   - Should women be written into the U. S. Constitution to have equal rights under the law?
   - Should the legal age for driving be changed in your state?
   - Should communities be allowed to ban rock music concerts within city limits?
   - Should stores such as Wal-Mart be allowed to refuse to sell specific tapes/CDs because of content?
   - Should the grading system in your school be changed?
   - Should your student council be given more power in determining school policy?
   - Should your school's faculty and administration be allowed to censor school newspapers?
   - Should individuals and community groups be allowed to censor reading materials in schools and libraries?
3. Ask students to discuss the topic within their groups for 10 to 15 minutes.

Debriefing: The following questions might be considered during the discussion:
1. Did you ever feel you were not being understood?
2. What behaviors of other group members made you feel this way?
3. What did you do when you believed your message was misunderstood?
4. What other things could you have done?
5. What do you do when you don't understand another person's message?

Assessment: Ask each student to fill out the following Self-Evaluation Form and discuss it with you.

Self-Evaluation Form

Think about your behavior in your small group and explain on this form whether you believe it did or did not affect the group.

Behavior Strategy	Did Affect	Did Not
1. Speaking loudly and clearly enough to be heard	☐	☐
2. Providing a summary of my major points	☐	☐
3. Using examples to clarify my ideas	☐	☐
4. Disagreeing tactfully rather than belligerently	☐	☐
5. Listening carefully to what others said before responding	☐	☐
6. Nonverbally showing my interest by eye contact, posture, and/or gestures	☐	☐
7. List and describe other behaviors . . .		
_____	☐	☐
_____	☐	☐
_____	☐	☐
_____	☐	☐
_____	☐	☐
_____	☐	☐

ACTIVITY

1.15   It Just Sounds Pretty

Standard 7: Competent communicators demonstrate the ability to evaluate communication styles, strategies, and content based on their aesthetic and functional worth.

Grade Levels: 7–8

Description: This activity encourages students to better understand the aesthetics of communication by having them make critical judgments about poetry and writing based on a set of criteria they develop.

Objective: Students will identify and apply criteria to evaluate the function and aesthetics of communication styles, respect the right of others to differ in their evaluation of an aesthetic event, and define aesthetics.

Materials: Tape or CD player, pen/pencil

Procedure:
1. Define the term "aesthetics" (a sense of beauty) for students.

2. Ask students to write a definition of "beauty," describe something they think is beautiful and why they think so, and explain how that example fits with their definition.

3. Have students share their descriptions and examples in small groups.

4. Discuss with students how definitions, standards, and applications are different.

5. Draw discussion to the concept that communication can be evaluated for beauty. How people talk, their voices, language, singing, music, dance, film, and so forth are all examples of various forms of communication that can be judged on their aesthetic value.

6. Have groups of three to four students create a rubric for evaluating the aesthetic value of the poems or stories they like to read and listen to. Create a personal rubric as a model for the students. An example might be:

	Yes	No	Unclear
Does the poem's topic relate to the reader?	☐	☐	☐
Do the characters make believable choices?	☐	☐	☐
Do the words create strong pictures in the reader's mind?	☐	☐	☐

7. Have students bring in their favorite poem or story to class, or provide a variety of written examples for them.

8. Read the poems or stories, and have students evaluate them using their rubrics. Discuss differences among the rubrics and how they show differences in aesthetic standards. Show how students using the same rubric can evaluate the same writing differently. Students could also use their rubrics to evaluate their own writings.

Debriefing: Ask such questions as:

1. Did everyone evaluate the same poem or story the same way?

2. Why do people judge aesthetics so differently?

3. What implication does this have for communication for speakers? For listeners?

Assessment: Observe students as they participate in the discussion and use their rubrics. Look for an ability to create criteria for judgment and the ability to apply those to aesthetic events. Students should be able to describe how developing criteria and using standards relate to aesthetics and how each student may view a piece of communication differently. Students could also write out their answers to question #3 above.

ACTIVITY

1.16 | Haiku

Standard 7: Competent communicators demonstrate the ability to evaluate communication styles, strategies, and content based on their aesthetic and functional worth.

Grade Levels: 7–8, 9–10

Description: This oral-reading activity helps sensitize students to the feelings behind a message by having students read haikus aloud and make vocal choices. The choices should show the author's feelings to the audience and at the same time enhance the aesthetic quality of poetry.

Objective: Students will read haiku with feelings they think are appropriate and provide feedback to the readings of others.

Materials: Haikus, Haiku Reading Evaluation Form

Procedure: Pass out a selection of haikus to the class and have each student choose one to read. Two or more students may read the same haiku. Each student should try to read the poem in a way that re-creates the emotional tone the writer tried to capture.

Debriefing: Use the following questions to help the class discuss the readings:

1. What tone did you feel the reader created?
2. Did it seem appropriate to the haiku?
3. How else might the haiku be read? (If more than one student has chosen the same haiku, have them read one after the other and then discuss.)

Assessment: Use the Haiku Reading Evaluation Form to provide feedback to students.

Haiku Reading Evaluation Form

Reader's Name: _____

Emotional tone:

    Appropriate?   Yes   No

    Clearly expressed?   Yes   No

Comments:

_____

_____

_____

_____

Delivery:

Vocal delivery	1	2	3	4	5
Use of pauses	1	2	3	4	5
Gestures	1	2	3	4	5
Posture	1	2	3	4	5
Props (optional)	1	2	3	4	5
Enthusiasm/sincerity	1	2	3	4	5

Comments:

_____

_____

_____

_____

Scale:

  5 = Superior

  4 = Excellent

  3 = Good

  2 = Fair

  1 = Poor

ACTIVITY

1.17   And the *Other* Moral of the Story Is . . .

Standard 7: Competent communicators demonstrate the ability to evaluate communication styles, strategies, and content based on their aesthetic and functional worth.

Grade Levels: 9–10, 11–12

Description: In this activity, the teacher chooses and shows a feature film to illustrate communication analysis. Students will view and discuss a film such as *The Breakfast Club, Twelve Angry Men, Dead Poets Society, Roger and Me,* or another film of the teacher's choice. After discussing what the intended lesson or moral is, students consider and discuss other outcomes of the interpersonal interactions seen in the film.

Objective: Students will critically evaluate the outcomes of interpersonal interactions in films.

Materials: A copy of the film of choice, TV, VCR, or DVD player.

Procedure:
1. Choose a film and, after carefully previewing it, prepare questions for discussion of what students believe the intended message or lesson of the film might be. For example, if *The Breakfast Club* is used, students may be drawn into a discussion of how the intimate self-disclosure brings the five high school students from various social cliques together and helps them become aware of other groups. On the surface, the moral appears to be that self-disclosure is the key to interpersonal success.

2. After complete discussion, ask the students to consider alternate morals to the story. In *The Breakfast Club,* for instance, it is likely that the five students will return to their own cliques on Monday and re-engage in negative behaviors. The alternate moral of the story would then be that intimate self-disclosure with virtual strangers may be unwise. Asking students to consider the possible drawbacks of self-revealing communication exposes them to a broader understanding of the concept.

Debriefing: If you use *The Breakfast Club,* have students answer the following question in writing and/or in class discussion: *The Breakfast Club* portrays self-disclosure as positive, healthy, and constructive. Argue the opposite; develop a worst-case scenario of what could happen in the weeks following the detention session.

Assessment: Ask students to provide examples of other films that raise a great deal of interpersonal interaction, self-disclosure, and/or conflict, or ethical issues. Ask them to state their views and then look for and express the other side of the story, or the opposite perspective from the obvious one. If you view a film such as *Dead Poets Society,* you might ask students to take a villain/hero approach to the teacher's character. Have half the class take one perspective/side and the other half take the opposite side; give them questions before the film is viewed so they can be watching for evidence to support the view they have been assigned. Questions raised by both you and the students should demonstrate such communication concepts as perception, ethics, power, persuasion, and critical thinking.

ACTIVITY

1.18   Don't Judge Me by My Cover

Standard 8: Competent communicators demonstrate the ability to show sensitivity to the ethical issues associated with communication in a democratic society.

Grade Levels: 7–8, 9–10

Description: By having them dress "differently" for a day, this activity provides students direct experience with the role stereotypes play in communication.

Objective: Students will interpret the behavior of others who make stereotypical judgments and show willingness to see beyond stereotypes to seek individual worth.

Materials: None

Procedure:
1. Lead a discussion helping students to define cultural stereotypes; then help the class brainstorm various stereotypes perceived in their community. Examples may include punks, grunge, jocks, nerds, gangster, redneck, and so forth.
2. Have students select a stereotype different from their typical style.
3. Name a day "Stereotype Day." Ask students to dress in their designated stereotypical style for the day, noting how others, particularly strangers, communicate with them.
4. At the next class meeting, have students share their observations and draw conclusions regarding ways to communicate with ethical sensitivity.

Debriefing: Use questions such as the following to help students process the experience and relate it to communication:
1. How did people communicate with you?
2. How did it make you feel?
3. Did your communication style change as a result of your new identity?
4. How you ever judged someone based on a stereotype? Why?
5. How does stereotyping affect communication in society?

Assessment: Students can write a short personal essay or journal entry describing their experiences and lessons learned about the relationship between communication and stereotypes. The class, as a whole or individually, can create bumper sticker slogans admonishing people not to "judge books by their covers."

ACTIVITY

1.19   What's Your View?

Standard 8:   Competent communicators demonstrate the ability to show sensitivity to the ethical issues associated with communication in a democratic society.

Grade Levels: 9–10, 11–12

Description: Groups of students prepare for a panel discussion involving city officials. Students complete all arrangements and follow-up for the panel and then discuss their responses to the panelists.

Objective: Students will formulate questions to obtain information about their city and/or their public officials and to become aware of the ethical issues involved in democracy.

Materials: None

Procedure:

1. Invite city officials—such as the mayor, the chief of police, the fire chief, the prosecuting (county or city) attorney, and/or the superintendent of schools—to a meeting.

2. Have students prepare invitations, hospitality, publicity, and a student panel to interview the officials, serve refreshments, and write follow-up notes of appreciation.

3. In preparation for the panel, discuss as a class the role communication plays in the job descriptions of the officials and what ethical issues each might face.

4. Have each student list five or more questions she would like to ask the guest.

5. Divide the class into groups of five to seven members. Each group selects four to six questions from the group members. In addition, each group selects a representative to be on the class committee to review all questions for inclusion in a master list for the panel to use.

Debriefing: After the panel, consider the following questions during the discussion:

1. What did you learn about the workings of our city?

2. Do you agree with the views expressed? Why or why not? Which views were most memorable for you?

3. What changes do you think the various officials need to make in their policies? Why?

4. Which policies ought to remain the same? Why?

5. If you were one of the officials, how would you change things? Why?

6. What role did ethics play in the officials' explanations and responses?

7. What role does communication play in their jobs?

Assessment: Assess students on how well they completed their individual assignments, how well they listened to the information presented, and how well they utilized the information in forming their own views and opinions.

SPEAKING

TEACHING ACTIVITIES FOR NCA STANDARDS 9-12

Introduction

For over 2,500 years, people have studied the art of public speaking—no wonder, since public speaking is a liberal art that frees and empowers people. Studying public speaking teaches students the essential skills of critical thinking, clear self-expression, research, audience analysis, and organization. Students also learn that their rhetorical choices have consequences and begin to understand their ethical responsibilities in speaking situations. Such skills are useful in both educational and career settings. In addition, such skills make for articulate citizens who understand the power of the spoken word.

The Standards

This unit includes teaching activities for the four standards to promote improved speaking skills. The standards in this category help students better understand the speaking process, adapt messages to specific situations and audiences, use language appropriately, and manage anxiety. They help students recognize the complexity of the process involved in public presentations. All activities were selected to demonstrate that speaking situations and settings vary and that an effective speaker needs to make good choices about topics, organization, language, and delivery when preparing individual and group presentations.

2.1 Delivery Cards

Standard 9: Competent speakers demonstrate knowledge and understanding of the speaking process.

Grade Levels: 7–8, 9–10

Description: This activity focuses on both delivery and topic. Students present an impromptu speech on a topic they draw (or are given), using a poor delivery style. "Delivery cards" may be used after the teacher has provided information on the process of speaking, including effective delivery. While the focus is on delivery, the activity also helps students understand the impact of delivery on the listener.

Objective: Students will recognize and explain how ineffective delivery can negatively impact the message they are trying to convey.

Materials: Pack of delivery cards on paper or index cards (one card for each delivery style or for each student in class and one extra for the teacher to use as an example). Each delivery card has two pieces of information. The top of the card describes a poor delivery style (such as speaking too quickly). The bottom of the card gives a topic for an impromptu speech (e.g., how to tie shoelaces). (See the sample delivery cards at the end of this activity.)

Procedure:
1. After introducing the subject of speech delivery to the students, explain that all students will help demonstrate the impact of poor delivery skills on the topic, the speaker, and the listeners. Ask for a set number of volunteers, or set up an order for speaking.

2. Give each student a card randomly selected from the pack. Caution students to keep the topic and style a secret to see whether listeners can guess the problem. Be sure to randomly draw from the deck for students so they don't think you have targeted them for a delivery problem they have.

3. Let students think about the topic for about a minute and then have them present a one-minute impromptu "speech" on the topic, using the delivery style they drew.

4. Stop the speaker after a minute, and ask the class what is wrong with the delivery style being used. Continue the activity until all volunteers (or all students) have presented. Students usually have a lot of fun with this learning game, and some presenters may "ham it up" a bit. By the end of the activity, the group should have a clearer idea of how delivery can impact even the best of messages and how each topic brings with it specific delivery demands.

Debriefing: Discuss why the message about the topic was hindered by the delivery style by asking students to:

1. identify why the delivery interfered with the message

2. explain what they think would be a better way to present messages

3. share what they will remember about this activity

Assessment: Assign groups and instruct each group to construct a message and choose a delivery for an effective presentation. Each group member will have a specific role to play (for example, one student introduces the speaker, one is the speaker, one explains why the group choose the message, one explains why the group thought the delivery was a good one, etc.). You may also play a videotaped speech that demonstrates several aspects of poor delivery and ask students to critique the speech. You might wish to identify specific criteria so the students know what to look for: appropriate rate of speech, good use of pauses, clearly understandable words, good eye contact, effective gestures and body movement, etc.). If you wish to have students provide feedback to others when presentations are made, ask them to discuss what they would tell the speaker about improving the speech.

Sample Delivery Cards

Problem: Speak too quickly Topic: How to tie shoelaces	Problem: Use too many big hand gestures Topic: Explain why using the correct word is important
Problem: Avoid looking at the audience (look at the floor) Topic: Explain why courtesy is important on the playground	Problem: Speak too slowly Topic: Tell your listeners about an exciting thing that happened (on a vacation, in a sports event on television, etc.)
Problem: Speak without pauses Topic: Give suggestions about how to stay calm when you have a speech to give	Problem: Play with your notecard while speaking Topic: Describe a scene from a recent movie
Problem: Use too many pauses or use pauses in inappropriate places Topic: Describe a funny event you saw on television	Problem: Speak in a monotone Topic: Tell about an exciting ride on a bicycle, a motorcycle, or an amusement park ride

ACTIVITY

2.2 | Look Who's Listening: The Importance of Subaudiences in Public Speaking

Standard 9: Competent speakers demonstrate knowledge and understanding of the speaking process.

Grade Levels: 7–8, 9–10

Description: This activity is designed to help students understand the complex nature of the speaking process. It also emphasizes that speakers need to make effective choices and adapt both message and delivery to the interests of the listener.

Objective: Students will experience and plan for subaudiences in public speaking situations.

Materials: An audio- or videotaped speech or presentation. Examples include:

> The slow-motion montage of Christa McAuliffe's life shown on television the night of January 28, 1986
>
> Nixon's "Checkers" speech
>
> A documentary video on the death of Jackie Kennedy Onassis or John Lennon
>
> An MTV video
>
> A great play from a sports event
>
> A radio or television commercial
>
> A segment from a soap opera or sitcom
>
> A news report or a segment from a newsmagazine program, such as *20/20* or *60 Minutes*
>
> A videotaped speech from a high school speech class or forensics competition

While these examples come from a variety of sources and include nonpublic speaking examples, the right segments from a soap opera or sitcom, for example, may provide insights into the public presentation process.

Procedure:
1. After explaining to students what is involved in speaking to an audience, use this activity to help students see the varied and dynamic reactions by different people to the same taped event.

2. Play a short segment of the tape (about two minutes). When the segment is over, ask the students to write down how they feel.

3. Let all students express their personal responses to the tape. As students reveal their reactions, the nature of subaudiences and the importance of anticipating them should become clear. If one set of frames can evoke such a wide range of emotions, then certainly a speech's examples, quotations, choice of wording, and so forth might do the same.

4. Explain that public speakers need to anticipate real-life, active, diverse listeners; envision a variety of subaudiences; and plan for them. A subaudience may be adapted to or deliberately excluded from the remarks but should not be ignored.

Debriefing: Discuss the various responses to the tape. List each response on the board or on a transparency, and count the number of different responses to the same event. Let students discuss differing presentations and their own responses to them. Then, summarize and synthesize their responses.

Assessment:

1. Let students respond to the question, "What have you learned about speaking and storytelling from this activity?"

2. Ask students to think of situations in which they were speakers and did not understand the responses of some of their listeners.

3. Ask students to think about why there are so many different responses to the same event.

4. Ask students to identify how they think this activity will affect them as they prepare for their own speeches or presentations for class and in the future.

5. Ask students to identify their own unique perspectives and how those affect them as listeners.

ACTIVITY

2.3   Pointers for Polished Public Speaking

Standard 9:   Competent speakers demonstrate knowledge and understanding of the speaking process.

Grade Levels: 9–10, 11–12

Description: This activity requires students to think about what is wrong with another person's speech style and delivery. Students gain an opportunity to focus on effective speech content and delivery to learn more about the speaking process.

Objective: Students will develop and deliver polished public speeches/presentations.

Materials: None. You may wish, however, to create a handout, transparency, chalkboard/porcelain board list, or PowerPoint® slides listing the 12 statements below so that students will be able to both see and hear the examples.

Procedure: Ask students to identify what is wrong in each statement below and to describe what the recommended public speaking procedure would be.

1. The speaker, John Smith, begins speaking before being fully settled at the speaker's stand.
2. John bluntly announces his thesis statement in his opening sentence.
3. Previous to stating his thesis, he announces his speech title.
4. John covers five major points. It doesn't become apparent that this is the number he is covering until near the end of his speech.
5. John gives only an outline of the last two of his main points.
6. The statement of John's last major outline point is the point at which he ends his speech and sits down.
7. Every so often, as John is thinking of what to say next, he fills in with "you know," "okay," or "and stuff."
8. In several places, John uses slang expressions. For instance, he says, "The cops had a blast at the party."
9. As John gives a major point of information, almost without taking time to breathe he moves on to his next point.
10. John uses many vocabulary words of a specialized technical field while addressing an audience not schooled in the technical field.
11. John has about five pages of notes for his delivery of this extemporaneous speech.
12. Numerous quotations, statistics, and undetailed examples are John's major forms of supporting materials.

Debriefing: The content and/or delivery problems represented by each statement are provided below:

1. The speaker should take 10 to 20 seconds to get settled at the speaker's stand. This helps to establish appropriate pacing and a reasonable rate of delivery, allows the audience to focus its full attention on the speaker, and makes for an impressive and strong beginning. It may also prevent listeners from missing a key word or two in the opening sentences.
2. Build up to the announcement of the topic by using an example, a description, or narration that leads logically to the topic announcement. The speaker receives the strongest audience attention during the first seconds of the speech. This is why speakers need an interesting beginning and may use suspense before revealing the

specific topic. As soon as the topic or thesis is announced, the audience's attention may wane. If the introduction is well developed and interesting, audience members are more likely to refocus their attention again, quickly.

3. Generally, speakers do not announce a speech title. A title weakens the introduction by making the topic immediately clear. It is also considered poor etiquette in most situations to announce a title. (One might be required to state a title in a speech contest, however. In contests and regarding speeches for civic clubs, one usually supplies a printed title in advance for the program listing or for publicity purposes. It is also appropriate to list a title at the top of the speech outline that is not actually stated when delivering the address.)

4. John needs to preview his structure at the end of his introduction by announcing his thesis or topic and the number of subtopics he will cover. Usually, he would list each subtopic as well, unless an important suspense value is to be served by not revealing the exact subtopics at this point.

5. John should detail thoroughly all the major points of his speech. If he doesn't have time to do this with the last point or two, he should omit those points from his speech. Without thorough detailing, a major point will be vague, unclear, and quickly forgotten by the audience.

6. John needs to develop a definite conclusion after his last main point is covered. He might review his thesis and/or major points, suggest appropriate audience action, or give a memorable quotation that sums up his speech. The speaker might actually say "in conclusion" or "in summary" to prevent an abrupt ending and then finish with a memorable last line.

7. These are common pause fillers. Speakers should stop to think about what they want to say, using silence instead of filling in with these distracting expressions.

8. Generally, speakers use standard grammar in a public speech unless quoting someone else's actual or reconstructed dialogue.

9. John needs to slow his overall speaking rate, taking time to breathe properly. Otherwise, he will be worn-out as well as have poor pacing in his presentation. Audience members will also have difficulty understanding and retaining his speech materials because they don't have time to reason along with the speaker.

10. John should translate as many technical words as he can to everyday vocabulary. Those that cannot be translated should be defined carefully.

11. John has a total or partial manuscript. This is likely to cause a boring reading instead of a conversational presentation. Preferably, he should have only a couple of note cards containing a brief outline.

12. Too many facts and statistics in one speech can cause "information overload." The audience ends up neither understanding nor remembering much. Quotations can be impressive if one or two are used. A speech composed largely of quoted material, however, is neither interesting nor effective, may be boring, or may sound as though the speaker has few original ideas. A detailed example (a full paragraph) adds more clarity and interest than an undetailed (phrase or sentence) example. Along with good detailed examples, however, one or two additional undetailed ones can add additional weight of evidence for a point or argument without taking much time to deliver.

Assessment: If you have access to audio- or videotaped speeches from former students, forensics students, or even famous speakers, have students listen to one of the tapes and evaluate how well the speaker followed the pointers for polished public speaking. You may create your own evaluation sheets for student use in evaluating the presented speeches or use one of the evaluation criteria sheets in Unit 5.

ACTIVITY

2.4 Who Is the Listener?

Standard 9: Competent speakers demonstrate knowledge and understanding of the speaking process.

Grade Levels: 9–10, 11–12

Description: This set of assignments covers several days and may be used at differing times throughout the academic year. The activity allows teacher and students to explore the role of the audience in the communication process. By presenting several messages for different listeners and different situations, students adapt their language, style, and delivery to meet the various situations. You may use the full series of assignments or pick as many as you think will help your students understand the speaking process.

Objective: Students will speak and write for specific audiences.

Materials: None

Procedure: *Assignment 1:* Students introduce themselves (this is the "real" me) using some criteria or characteristics the teacher chooses (hobbies, favorite reading genre, favorite kind of movie, heroes, what they would do if they were to win the lottery, etc.) in a relaxed atmosphere—students remain seated and are conversational. They should receive points for the assignment, simply for completing the task. Ask each student to listen carefully to all introductions because their next assignment will be related to a particular student whom they have met through these preliminary introductions.

Assignment 2: For homework, each student writes an informal letter to another student of her choice—perhaps someone they do not know but would like to know better (don't let good friends be partners for this assignment). This writing assignment asks them to identify a specific person as the reader, based on statements made in the earlier assignment. In the letters, students provide additional information about their own interests and ask and answer questions that were not answered in the brief introduction in Assignment 1. This exercise, combined with the previous assignment, enhances listening skills by responding to the previous activity (Assignment 1) and adding information not covered in that initial activity. It also helps reduce anxiety that could hamper speaking ability for the rest of the semester.

Assignment 3: Now that they are better acquainted with others in the class, students should feel comfortable working in pairs (possibly with the individual they chose in Assignment 2) on this next assignment, a "Present/Accept Award Speech." The pairs decide who will present and who will accept the award, and they discuss the award itself. Allow them to chose their own awards, real or fictional. They also must predetermine their audience. Students should think about their classmates as one audience but should also consider other "assumed audiences" for the award speeches. For example, students may consider giving the presentation/award acceptance speeches for a local rotary or veterans group since those organizations provide scholarships and awards for students and community members. Students write two-minute presentations/acceptances and rehearse aloud with each other for content, time, and a conversational voice—all appropriately adapted for their chosen audience.

Assignment 4: Ask students to choose a piece of children's literature to be presented as an interpretive reading. Remind the students to think about "bringing the story to life" for their listeners with lots of vocal variety and the appropriate amount of enthusiasm and energy for the topic. Inform students that their audience is a class of elementary school children (you might wish to specify a particular grade level) and that they must demonstrate audience awareness by predetermining the appropriateness of both their selection and delivery (props, facial expressions, movements, gestures) for this audience. Presentations should be four to six minutes long.

Assignment 5: Students select a former U. S. president and write a campaign speech to be delivered to members of the class as the opposite political party. Ask students to sign up for their choices, and allow only two students per president. This exercise provides a different audience analysis challenge and also requires research skills. Seven- to 10-minute presentations are made. Students must conduct research and use at least three different sources/references for this assignment.

Assignment 6: For this final assignment, students select a controversial topic/issue about which to write and speak. After they sign up for their topics and the position they wish to defend, inform them that they must take the opposite stand. Tell students to assume that the audience holds their original view and challenge them to persuade the audience to change their perspective in a 10- to 12-minute presentation. This assignment helps students learn "to see the other side," requires research skills (ask for at least five different sources), and puts a unique twist on audience analysis as students analyze the layers of their own beliefs that are now presumed to belong to their listeners.

Debriefing: After each assignment, discuss what happened with the students. Students need to be able to identify similarities and differences between the various assignments.

Assessment: Assign varied audiences by having students choose a different topic and present another speech. Provide students numerous opportunities to adapt their messages to different audiences throughout the academic term. Remind them prior to formal presentations and speeches that audience analysis is always an important assessment criterion. You may also create your own evaluation criteria sheets or use or adapt one of the evaluation criteria forms found in Unit 5 for various aspects of the assignments.

A C T I V I T Y

2.5 Tell and Show; Listen and Draw

Standard 10: Competent speakers demonstrate the ability to adapt communication strategies appropriately and effectively according to the needs of the situation and setting.

Grade Levels: 7–8

Description: In this activity, students listen to others and respond to their messages. The activity is designed to reinforce students' ability to adapt messages to specific audiences and to make students aware of the kinds of choices they need to make when presenting their ideas to others. In addition, the impact of the message's organization will be reinforced.

Objective: Students will explain how to adapt communication strategies to meet the needs of the situation and setting.

Materials: Paper, crayons/markers

Procedure: Tell students they will have an opportunity to share with the class a possession of importance to them. The possession should fit in a paper bag and be able to be brought to school. Students also need to have a mind-set for listening to their classmates.

1. Prepare for the lesson two or three days before the activity is scheduled.

2. Ask students to bring with them to class, in a paper bag, an object important to them. Preschedule the speaking order, because no more than three to five students should present their objects on any given day.

3. Each day, announce the day's speaking order (you might have students present in reverse alphabetical order or alphabetical order, have students draw for order, or randomly assign speaking order).

4. Ask students to carefully consider how they present their objects. They should identify some main areas of description: what the object feels like if touched, what its uses are, where one may find it in a typical house, where the student keeps it, how the student treats it, and so forth.

5. Distribute paper and crayons to students.

6. Give students two or three minutes each to describe orally, without naming the object, what they brought in their bags. The goal is to give enough information so the class can accurately envision the object.

7. Based on the students' descriptions, ask the other students to draw what they think is in the bag.

8. After the day's speakers have shared information about the objects they brought, ask listeners what they thought was in each bag and have them share their drawings. Begin processing the lesson by asking the questions below.

9. Continue the activity on other days with the remainder of the students.

Debriefing: First, look at the pictures students drew and find out what they represent and why. Then ask such questions as:

1. What could the teller do to be more specific?

2. What would help the listener get a more accurate idea about what is in the bag (gestures, words, more information)?

3. What could the listener do to get a better idea about what is in the bag?

Tell students you will be looking in future sessions to see that their work incorporates the suggestions established for both speakers and listeners in this activity.

Assessment: Evaluate students on (1) adherence to guidelines, (2) participation in the activity, and (3) soundness of the contributions they offer during the processing of the activity.

ACTIVITY

2.6 My Mind's Made Up; Don't Confuse Me with the Facts

Standard 10: Competent speakers demonstrate the ability to adapt communication strategies appropriately and effectively according to the needs of the situation and setting.

Grade Levels: 9–10, 11–12

Description: Students use print and nonprint editorials to distinguish between facts and opinions and between informative and persuasive messages. Critical analysis of editorials and opinion pieces will help students differentiate the strategies used to communicate truth and fiction, fact and opinion, and information and persuasion.

Objective: Students will use critical thinking skills and be able to distinguish between informative and persuasive messages in print and nonprint media. They will also be able to clearly differentiate between facts and opinions.

Materials: Bring to class a variety of opinion pieces (including Web sites, radio, television, or even performances) or ask students to search for an editorial or opinion piece with which they strongly agree or strongly disagree. Either way, provide copies of these opinion pieces for students to use in this activity. For background reading, choose any one of a number of textbooks to provide basic information about the concepts of fact, opinion, and informative and persuasive messages. Some examples include *Person to Person* (Galvin and Book, 1990); *The Basics of Speech* (Galvin and Cooper, 1999); and *Oral Communication: Speaking and Listening* (Hunsaker, 1990).

Procedure: 1. Review facts, opinions, informative messages, and persuasive messages in class.

2. Assign students to read and review several opinion pieces from the Internet, television, radio, recordings, performances, newspaper editorials, magazine editorials, letters to the editor, or the "My Turn" section of *Newsweek* and the like. (This may be given as homework or as an in-class writing and discussion session.) Instruct students to complete the assignment and bring the one or two "best" opinion pieces to class with them.

3. Ask students to choose one piece and analyze it to determine the following:

   a. Is the piece all fact, all opinion, or a combination? How do you know?

   b. Is the piece primarily informative or persuasive? How do you know?

   c. What is the argument made in this piece?

   d. With what do you agree? Why?

   e. With what do you disagree? Why?

   f. How well did the author make the case of the claim or argument made?

   g. How well did the author support the argument?

   h. If you were going to make this argument, how would you change it?

Debriefing: Discuss the analysis of the editorials with the whole class. Ask students the following questions:

1. How did you arrive at the decisions you did?

2. What criteria did you use to make your choices?

3. What would the author need to do to get you to change your mind?

4. How did you decide the purpose of the message?

5. What can we learn from analyzing opinion pieces and editorials?

As a follow-up activity, students should select one letter or editorial and prepare a response to it, or they could write their own letters to the editor. They should identify the informative and persuasive strategies included in their own writing/speaking. After analyzing the opinion pieces, students should discuss their findings using the following questions:

1. Which messages were effective? Why?

2. Which messages were ineffective? Why?

3. How could the ineffective messages be made more effective?

Assessment: Each student should submit a written summary of the observations described in the "Procedure" section. A copy of the editorials, letters, or transcripts should accompany the analysis. Evaluate each summary on the student's ability to distinguish between persuasive and informative messages and between facts and opinions and to analyze the effectiveness of each. Remind students that they are consumers of messages and need to be aware of the communication strategies people employ in their messages. Create or bring in other examples of editorials or opinions, and ask students to critique their messages in a full class discussion. You might want to tape a noncontroversial episode of the *Oprah Winfrey Show* or a similar production to discuss. If you have access to some advertising award winners, this would provide another activity for students to analyze how others adapt communication strategies for specific situations and settings.

ACTIVITY

2.7   Using the Internet as an Information Source

Standard 10:   Competent speakers demonstrate the ability to adapt communication strategies appropriately and effectively according to the needs of the situation and setting.

Grade Levels: 10–12 (with adaptations for the specific level)

Description: This activity gives students practice using the Internet and evaluating the resources.

Objective: Students will develop critical and evaluative skills of Internet sources and ultimately learn to use credible sources for support of messages.

Materials: www.library.cornell.edu/okuref/research.webeval.html
www.library.ucla.edu/libraries/college/help/critical/index.htm
www.improbable.com/airchives/classical/cat/cat.html
Other research articles or Web sites may also be used.
Or, provide hard copies or a transparency of the Web pages. The checklist for Internet sources (see next page) should be given to each student.

Procedure: This activity is meant to supplement the standard discussion about the credibility and reliability of sources, specifically targeting the use of Internet sources for a communication assignment.

1. Display the Web pages and go over them with the entire class, or have students work on their own as homework. Students need to go over the Cornell and UCLA sites and then read the article in the final site. The first two sites are tutorials; the Cornell site offers tips on both Internet and non-Internet information sources, and the UCLA site includes a series of questions developed by librarian Esther Grassian that Web researchers should ask about sources. The final site is one entitled "Feline Reactions to Bearded Men." The article reads as if it were a scholarly article, but as students begin to apply the questions regarding reliability and credibility to this Internet source, they find how utterly ridiculous the source is! For those with limited Web access, instructors can provide a copy of the feline article for students to read or put it on a transparency or projector for students to read along.

2. As students read "Feline Reactions to Bearded Men," have them apply the "Internet Sources" checklist to the article.

Debriefing: Discuss students' perceptions after completing the assignment. Generally, following the completion of this exercise, students will be less likely to use questionable Web-based information as part of their assignments.

Assessment: Ask students to evaluate the Web sources they use and include that assessment with their reference pages. You can also administer a classroom assessment instrument for students to rate their understanding of course objectives and principles. Using a Likert-like scale (1 is "strongly agree" and 5 is "strongly disagree"), have students respond to these statements:

1. The discussion of Internet sources and how to evaluate them has increased my ability to carefully analyze sources.

2. I know how to find sources for my speeches from the Internet and how to evaluate their credibility.

Checklist: Internet Sources

1. What is the site's purpose?

   _____

2. Will its information be unbiased?

   _____

3. Who sponsors the site?

   _____

4. What are the organization's values or goals?

   _____

5. Can you contact the sponsors should questions arise?

   _____

6. Is the information in the site well documented?

   _____

7. Does it provide citations to sources used in obtaining the information?

   _____

8. Are individual articles signed or attributed?

   _____

9. When was it published? Is the date of the last revision posted somewhere on the page?

   _____

10. What are the author's credentials?

    _____

11. Is the author cited frequently in other sources?

    _____

12. How does the value of the Web-based information you've found compare with other available sources, such as print?

    _____

(Developed by David Boraks (March 22, 1997), *Amarillo Globe News,* p. 18A.)

ACTIVITY

2.8 | Transitional Stories

Standard 11: Competent speakers demonstrate the ability to use language that clarifies, persuades, and/or inspires while respecting differences in listeners' backgrounds (race, ethnicity, age, etc.).

Grade Levels: 9–10

Description: Students use a series of transition words as they create a story together.

Objective: Students will understand how to use transition words in a speech.

Materials: A list of different transition words and phrases (see sample)

Procedure:
1. Create a list of transition words and phrases (for example, *likewise, similarly, another*) and organize them according to specific categories (comparison, contrast, etc.).
2. Hand out the list to students.
3. Tell students that everyone will be creating a story orally by having each class member contribute a sentence or two that includes one of the transitions from the list.
4. Begin the story with an exciting introduction that allows students to add their own creative additions. One example of an introduction begins with a person walking along the beach and stumbling over an old green bottle that contains a secret message inside.
5. Students continue the story by adding their own sentences with transition words.
6. Discuss the activity.
7. Complete the activity again on another day to help students use transitions more easily.

Debriefing: Ask the following questions:
1. What did the transitions tell you?
2. Were they easy to hear?
3. What did you think about when you heard one of the words or phrases?
4. Did the list help you listen better for the connections between the ideas?

Assessment: Ask students such questions as:
1. What did you learn from this activity? Why?
2. How much smoother was the story when people remembered to use transitions? Tape-record a speech that contains few transitions (or give the speech to students in a written form). Ask them to supply the needed transitions.
3. Why are transitions important?
4. When should we use transitions?
5. Ask students to create and discuss a list of transitions relevant to specific situations (e.g., transitions appropriate for a speech of introduction, for an award presentation, for an award acceptance, for a speech on technology, for a speech describing an event, a persuasive speech, a how-to speech, a comparison-contrast speech, etc.). Ask the rest of the class if those transitions would help them, as listeners, keep track of speech content.

Sample Transition Words and Phrases

After all	In order to	On the other hand
Again	In other words	Otherwise
And then	In particular	Presently
Because	In short	Similarly
Besides	In spite of	Since
Briefly	Instead of	Still
But	In the meantime	Then
Consequently	Later	Thereafter
Different from	Likewise	Therefore
Finally	Moreover	Thus
Furthermore	Naturally	To illustrate
Hence	Nevertheless	To summarize
However	Next	Unlike
In conclusion	Notwithstanding	While
In contrast	Of course	Yet

ACTIVITY

2.9 Word Power

Standard 11: Competent speakers demonstrate the ability to use language that clarifies, persuades, and/or inspires while respecting differences in listeners' backgrounds (race, ethnicity, age, etc.).

Grade Levels: 9–10, 11–12

Description: This exercise allows groups of students to create a nonsense language and demonstrate how their language works.

Objective: Students will identify specific instances of the power of words/language and analyze the functions of words in a particular situation.

Materials: A list of specific situations from which students choose their task (selling an item, buying an item, handing someone an object, putting something away, etc.)

Procedure:
1. Without telling the class what you are doing, give a series of quick commands, such as, "Tania, open the door so we can have some air in here!" "Juan, would you come here, please?" "Class, open your books to page 20."

2. Explore with the students how and why they responded to the verbal commands given.

3. List student reactions on the board.

4. Extend the discussion by asking for other examples of how words control actions and manipulate feelings in students' lives outside the classroom.

5. Make a list of situations in which this manipulation is especially direct—for example, requesting that food be passed, selling an object, or making a purchase.

6. Divide the class into small groups and have each group choose one situation from the list. Ask each group to create a nonsense language (you might give the example of pig Latin or create your own nonsense examples, such as "oomlow satay zib possa" for "please pass the potatoes" or "pod wimmel oxsa glumfor" for "I wish to buy the blanket" or "Zapata nogos rekovor" for "this painting is not for sale"). The language should have no more than 25 very specific words, designed to permit the speaking necessary to complete the task. Limit the time to about 20 minutes (less if students complete their work more quickly).

7. Have each group explain and demonstrate how their language works by showing its pronunciation, rate, and inflections of their language, using peers who were not in their group. For example, choose one of the sentences above and explain it as you would have the students do.

8. Discuss together the reasons for including the words that appear on the list of each group.

Debriefing: Ask students such questions as:
1. What kinds of words did you make up for carrying out the tasks? (Possible answers might be nouns, verbs, connection words, descriptors, etc.)

2. What rules did you use to make up words that could be said?

3. What use of tone and gesture did you make to put your idea across?

4. How might your tone or gesture vary with a much younger person? A much older person? An international student (an exchange student or an immigrant)? Another student? A teacher? A police officer? Demonstrate.

5. What kinds of words carry the power of command? How do tone and gesture reinforce that power?

Assessment: From time to time, refer to this activity and ask students to compare this activity to other specific language-based activities you use in the classroom. Remind students of the need to use more than words to create meanings. Use this activity as a basis for a test or quiz question about use of language appropriate to situations and contexts. Remind students that the evaluation criteria used for their presentations include the language choices they make in their presentations.

ACTIVITY

2.10   Using Group Speaking to Overcome Anxiety

Standard 12:   Competent speakers demonstrate the ability to manage or overcome communication anxiety.

Grade Levels: 7–8

Description: This is a group activity designed to help students create messages and manage their anxiety about presentations. It emphasizes both critical and creative thinking.

Objective: Students will overcome communication anxiety.

Materials: Two pictures of items students would find interesting or humorous, glued on 8.5 × 11-inch paper. Label each picture as follows (see the sample cards on the following page):

> Example : Picture of a tank
>
> Product : TANK II
>
> Producer : Ford Motor Company
>
> Proposition : Everyone should own the car of the future: TANK II

> Example : Picture of a rundown house or cabin
>
> Product : QUAINT LEISURE ABODE
>
> Producer : Handyperson's Special Offers
>
> Proposition : You, too, can own a Handyperson's Special: QUAINT LEISURE ABODE

Procedure: 1. Present a brief discussion comparing and contrasting how persuasive speaking differs from informative speaking. Emphasize the need for facts and opinions to support the proposition (the claim of the speech, or what you're trying to get the listeners to accept). Examples of persuasive speeches should be included in the discussion. Sales talks, a familiar example, may be the first type of persuasive speech students prepare.

2. After the preliminary discussion, the class should be divided into groups of four or five. Give each group two pictures of items they may sell. The group will select one of the two products to sell.

3. Each group will have 20 minutes to compose a persuasive speech outline that includes the following:

   I. Introduction

   II. The proposition—what result do you wish? Or what is it you wish the listeners to believe or do?

   III. Facts (created by students)

   A. Name of product

   B. Who makes the product

   C. How the product works

   D. Care of the product

   E. Cost of the product

F. Where and how to purchase the product

G. Any additional information deemed helpful by the group

IV. Opinions

A. Why it should be owned

B. Why it is considered better than other similar products

C. Quotations from "authorities" (group members)

V. Conclusions

4. Each group has five minutes to deliver the speech composed by the group. Every member of the group must present a part of the speech.

Debriefing: After each presentation, ask:

1. Would you buy this product? Why or why not?

2. If you weren't convinced to buy this product, what could the group have said to convince you?

When all of the speeches have been presented, ask:

1. Were you more comfortable writing and presenting the speech as a group rather than by yourself? Why or why not?

2. How might you use a group of your peers when preparing a speech? [Ask them for help in preparing the speech and practice your speech by presenting it to them prior to the class as a whole.]

Assessment: Assess the speeches using the persuasive speech evaluation form in Unit 5. Have listeners identify strengths of and needed repairs for the speeches presented.

ACTIVITY

2.11 Choral Oral Literacy

Standard 12: Competent speakers demonstrate the ability to manage or overcome communication anxiety.

Grade Levels: 7–8, 9–10

Description: This choral speaking activity can help students overcome their fear of speaking while experimenting with some dynamics of vocal delivery. The procedure is easy and fun for the instructor and students.

Objective: Students will overcome speech anxiety and improve vocal delivery skills in a public speaking setting.

Materials: None. Teachers may wish to have the list of words and phrases on the chalkboard, on a transparency, on PowerPoint slides, or on a handout to help students both see and hear the words.

Procedure:
1. Early in the school year, address the need to overcome speech anxiety and to develop a dynamic conversational delivery. Emphasize that confidence and good delivery develop through practice and familiarity. Show videos of speakers who model sound principles of delivery.

2. Tell your students at the beginning of the class that they will engage in a brief classroom exercise called "Choral Oral Literacy." To help students overcome their initial fears of this assignment, assure them that everyone will perform the learning strategy together. If you are using a printed/displayed form of the words and phrases to be used, distribute it.

3. To begin the exercise, have the students stand. Show them how to develop proper posture by standing straight and tall but not rigid. Ask them to take a deep breath from way down in the abdomen, so that their tummies move out when they inhale and move in as they exhale. Model good breathing and speaking as you give the directions. Explain to the class that they are to mimic your delivery in volume, rate, tone, and pitch.

4. Start by speaking in short, vivid sentences. Model a dynamic conversational delivery.

5. State the sentence and ask students to imitate, exactly, what you say and do. (See the example dialogue on the following page.) Vary rate, volume, and pitch in an animated conversational tone. Develop a complete word picture or metaphor in one or two minutes.

6. The key to making this learning activity work is to enjoy it. Demonstrate a variety of language and delivery styles. Imitate your favorite speakers (e.g., Barbara Jordan, Winston Churchill, Ann Richards, Martin Luther King Jr., John Kennedy, Rudy Giuliani, Laura Bush, George W. Bush, Condoleeza Rice, Colin Powell, Oprah Winfrey).

7. Engage in this activity several times prior to formal presentations or speeches. On days of presentations, begin with this exercise to warm up the students' vocal cords and help them overcome last-minute jitters.

Sample Oral Literacy Dialogue

"Today!" [Wait while students respond.] *(Smile)* [Wait for students' smiles.]

"Today, there are clouds outside." *(Pause)*

"But while there are clouds in the sky . . ." *(Pause)*

"There is sunshine in our souls." *(Smile and Pause)*

"We are sometimes anxious about speaking in front of others." *(Pause)*

"It is natural to be concerned about what we say." *(Pause)*

"We want to do a good job when we speak." *(Pause) (Smile)*

"For we know that learning to speak will free our ideas from the prison of our fears." *(Pause)*

"We will not allow them to hold us back any longer." *(Pause)*

"And when we are free . . ." *(Pause)*

"Free of our fears . . ." *(Pause)*

"Free to share our thoughts, our feelings . . ." *(Pause)*

"Then we will be able to overcome the problems that our world must face together."

"We will be happy to share our ideas with others." *(Smile)*

Debriefing: Ask such questions as:

1. Did you enjoy imitating me (the speaker)?

2. Did you have fun doing the exercise?

3. Why or why not?

4. Did saying positive words about your anxieties help you to see that anxiety is natural?

5. Did the group activity help reduce your anxiety?

6. Does thinking like this help you realize that you can manage your anxieties about speaking?

7. As the exercise continued with everyone saying the same thing, did you feel less anxious?

8. What will you remember about this exercise?

9. Will remembering the exercise help you feel more positive the next time you have to speak?

Assessment: Explain that anxiety is a normal feeling, and ask students to identify how this activity helped them to be aware of ways to manage it.

Have students keep a journal in which they share their feelings about their speeches on the day of presentations. At the end of the year, have them summarize ways in which they have overcome their communication anxiety. At the beginning of the school year and again at the end, students may complete the Personal Report of Communication Apprehension included in Unit 5. They should be able to see their progress by examining their scores of this assessment instrument.

ACTIVITY

2.12 Reducing Speaking Anxiety Through Speech Preparation

Standard 12: Competent speakers demonstrate the ability to manage or overcome communication anxiety.

Grade Levels: 9–10, 11–12

Description: Students prepare speeches well in advance of the due date and practice delivering them in small groups.

Objective: Students will reduce their communication anxiety.

Materials: A list of evaluation criteria (or actual critique sheet) for each student

Procedure: This activity is completed a day or two prior to the delivery of the first speech and may be used prior to every formal speaking or presentation assignment. The exercise requires one complete class period. Students should be told that the rehearsal speech is not graded but that they will lose participation points if they do not engage in the activity.

1. Students are required to come to class prepared to rehearse their speeches.
2. The class is divided into groups with about four students per group. The groups are placed in different locations in the room.
3. Each student in a group rehearses the speech in front of the other group members. Group members provide feedback according to the specifics of the assignment. For the informative speech, you may wish to stress organization, language use, development of ideas, and/or introductions and conclusions. (See Unit Five for some possible evaluation criteria.)
4. If at all possible, ask a speech/debate student or other experienced speaker to serve as a facilitator within the groups.
5. Group members use the list of criteria as the basis for their comments as they evaluate and offer suggestions for improvement.
6. Move throughout the room, monitoring groups and entering and exiting various groups.

Debriefing: Discuss the rehearsal situation at the end of the class by asking such questions as:

1. How do you now feel about the actual presentations?
2. How will you use your rehearsal comments to change your speeches or delivery?

Assessment: Ask students to identify how specific behaviors or feelings changed as a result of completing this assignment. Remind them that the criteria they use in rehearsals are the same you will use to grade the presentations. Use this activity to continue the discussion of anxiety management throughout the academic term.

ACTIVITY

2.13 | **Public Speaking:** Reducing Anxiety and Revealing a Process

Standard 12:   Competent speakers demonstrate the ability to manage or overcome communication anxiety.

Grade Levels: 9–10, 11–12

Description: In this activity, pairs of students interview each other and then introduce their partners to the class.

Objective: Students will overcome communication anxiety and gain an overview of the public speaking process.

Materials: None. For background, it would be helpful to read *Communication: Apprehension, Avoidance, and Effectiveness* (Richmond and McCroskey, 1995).

Procedure: This assignment serves both as an icebreaker and as an introduction to the public speaking process. Instead of a self-introductory speech at the beginning of the semester, have students design and deliver a speech that introduces another student. The assignment can be accomplished in two class sessions so that interest is maintained.

1. During the first session, pair students randomly to conduct mutual interviews. In addition to the basic information about each other, such as name, hobbies, and interests, encourage students to look for themes, such as how the interview partner overcame adversity, achieved a significant goal, or was changed by a meaningful experience.

2. Once the first student has gathered the information (usually 15 minutes is sufficient), have the students switch roles. Thus, each student has the opportunity to interview and to be interviewed.

3. Once both interviews are concluded, give the students 10 minutes at the end of class to organize the information into an outline.

4. During the next class session, ask each student to deliver a brief speech introducing his partner to the class.

5. Discuss with students the idea that as the audience members listen, the positive nonverbal communication they exhibit, such as smiles and nods, encourages the speakers. In addition, the discovery that there are more similarities than differences among the members of the audience further reduces their anxiety. It is always easier to speak to people who share interests. Teachers may wish to consider introductions of the speaker and the topic for successive rounds of speeches as well.

Debriefing: Remind students that it is normal to have some anxiety about the speaking process but that knowing who the listeners are and preparing wisely will help them in the speeches and presentations they make in class.

Lead students in a discussion about how this activity decreases anxiety. Help students gain a comprehensive overview of the important ingredients of the public speaking process: practice in the skills of interviewing, self-disclosing, listening, organizing information, and outlining. These skills provide the foundations on which the remainder of the course can be built.

Ask students to identify similarities and differences of students in the class.

Assessment: Make sure that the person making the introduction presented accurate information in the introduction by asking the persons being introduced to discuss the content of their introductions.

Give students the public speaking anxiety assessment instrument in Unit Five. If this is given twice during the year (once at the beginning of the term and again at the end of the term), students can "track" their level of communication anxiety.

Ask students to identify similar and different characteristics of class members identified in the introductions that might help speakers adapt their messages to this specific class. Ask students to identify two ways they might adapt speech content to specific characteristics of audience members.

LISTENING

unit 3

Introduction

The ability to listen effectively is important to succeeding in school, at work, and in relationships with family and friends. Research shows that we spend more time listening every day than we do in any of the other communication activities— reading, writing, and speaking. Although students begin school with some skills in listening (that is how they have learned up to this point), they still need training in listening if they are to become competent listeners—capable of understanding the listening process, using appropriate and effective skills for a given communication situation and setting, and identifying and managing barriers to listening.

Because listening and hearing are sometimes incorrectly considered synonymous, some teachers believe that if students can hear they can listen and that listening is an easy skill that should have been mastered before entering school. Such is not the case. Nor should teachers equate intelligence and listening. Many highly intelligent people are not effective listeners. Listening does not just happen; students must be taught the skills beginning with the first days of school and continuing throughout their educational careers. The basics that are taught in kindergarten should be reinforced and expanded during the subsequent years if students are to maintain and improve their skills.

The listening process is arguably one of the most overlooked of the communication process skills. The K–12 Standards (refer back to Figure I.1) identify three listening standards. They include knowledge and understanding of the listening process, the ability to use appropriate and effective listening skills for specific situations and settings, and the ability to identify and manage barriers to listening. The teaching activities included in this unit provide teachers with material to help students focus on the listening process and apply that knowledge in situations designed to help them develop effective listening skills. Teachers will find activities here to focus on listening skills as well as to reinforce competent listening.

61

The Listening Process

Wolvin and Coakley (1996) define listening as "the process of receiving, attending to, and assigning meaning to aural and visual stimuli." Although other definitions exist, this one is easy to understand and explains the process well. For example, the first component of the definition suggests that we first must receive (hear) aural and/or visual stimuli. Thus, hearing is the first component in the listening process and is distinguished from listening. Hearing is the physical process of picking up sounds or visual cues; listening includes the mental process involved in the rest of the definition.

Aural and visual stimuli are used because the listening process involves both. *Aural stimuli* include language sounds, words, vocal cues (such as volume and pitch), and other environmental sounds (such as bells and sirens). *Visual stimuli* can include a person's facial expressions, posture, or signs (either sign language or other recognized signs, such as a wave to tell someone hello or good-bye). Either the visual or the aural stimulus can serve as a trigger for listening to occur.

The second component in the listening process is *attending to the stimuli*. We all have been in situations where we have the radio or TV on but are not really paying attention to the noises coming from the equipment until something significant catches our attention and causes us to focus on the stimuli—a particular song, a name, or a newsworthy event, for example. This process of focusing our attention to the stimuli is the aspect of attending.

The third component in the listening process is *assigning meaning to the stimuli*. In the United States, we have a saying we apply to situations or messages that we don't understand. It is common to say that something was "Greek to me." If the code used by the sender is not the same as the one used by the receiver, then the meaning assigned to the message could be completely wrong—or "Greek" to the listener who doesn't understand it.

Effective Listening Skills

When attempting to list skills needed for effective listening, it is important to understand that the needed skills vary depending on the *purpose* for listening. We use different skills when we listen to learn than we do when we need to make critical decisions or when we are simply listening for enjoyment. Here are a few of the many purposes for listening and some of the related skills:

- *Listening for learning:* Skills include using memory techniques (for example, rhyming, acronyms, and acrostics), listening for main ideas (have students paraphrase a message to assess their understanding of it), and taking notes.

- *Empathetic listening:* Skills include focusing attention on the speaker (including looking at the speaker and resisting distractions) and reacting with appropriate verbal and nonverbal clues (including nodding one's head and displaying appropriate facial expressions).

- *Critical listening:* Skills include learning to make informed decisions or judgments based on what is heard (such as when children must evaluate requests made of them by peers and adults) and learning to understand, judge, and evaluate information (such as when we question what we read and see and evaluate sources). Critical listening is very important in student interactions with media.

Teachers and their students must learn to distinguish among different types of listening so that the appropriate skills can be learned and applied.

Listening Barriers

There are as many barriers to listening as there are listeners, and indeed each of us brings to bear our own unique barriers as a result of many factors. Following are some of the most common barriers that teachers can help students overcome:

- *Cultural background:* How we were raised, the beliefs of our families and friends, our experiences, and a multitude of other cultural factors influence how we listen and what meanings we attach to the messages we hear. Teachers must be sensitive to cultural differences when conveying messages and must help students understand how their reactions to messages are influenced by such factors.

- *Gender:* Research tells us that males and females listen differently. Females tend to be more aware of the mood of the conversation, and males tend to listen for facts. As teachers, we can train students to be concerned about both aspects when listening.

- *Age:* Generally, younger students have shorter attention spans; on the other hand, as a student's attention span lengthens, other factors related to age (e.g., spring fever!) may reveal themselves as barriers to listening.

- *Physical environment:* Factors such as ambient sound, temperature, comfort level, and light can act as barriers to effective listening. Teachers may have little control over many of these factors but should be aware of them and help students be aware of them. The physical time (e.g., early morning) of the message and time restraints (e.g., having only a set number of minutes to cover a lesson) can also affect listening.

- *Psychological status:* All of the above factors come into play when we consider whether students are ready and willing to listen. Students must be prepared to listen, and teachers may be able to help free them from stresses and mental distractions that can hinder effective listening.

- *Attitude:* We are all predisposed to listen and respond either positively or negatively to messages once we are aware of the topic. Our attitude is again affected by the factors listed above (our personal beliefs influence how we listen and react to a talk about racism, our age influences how we react to music, and so on). Teachers can set a positive tone for listening by encouraging students to listen with open minds and a desire to learn.

- *Desire to talk:* Add to the list the fact that most listeners would rather be talking than listening! As teachers, we must help our students understand when to talk and when to listen. A desire to listen is an important aspect of the process of becoming a better listener.

ACTIVITY

3.1   Let's Tell a Story

Standard 13: Competent listeners demonstrate knowledge and understanding of the listening process.

Grade Levels: 7–8, 9–10

Description: This activity helps students focus their attention during the telling of a story.

Objective: Students will practice active listening by focusing on a message and adapting to the listening situation.

Materials: Multicolored ball of yarn

Procedure:
1. Arrange the students in a circle and explain the "storyball":

   We will tell a story together. As the story begins, we unwind the yarn on the large ball and make a new ball of yarn. When the storyteller reaches a new color of yarn, the storyteller must stop and pass the yarn to the next person. The new storyteller then continues the story until she reaches a new color.

2. Continue the story until everyone has had a turn in telling the story. If necessary, rewind the yarn several times.

3. Make sure students are listening carefully to the other segments of the story and that their additions make sense.

4. You may want to stop occasionally and question students about the progress of the story and how new segments fit in with what came before.

5. Have students new to this activity tell a familiar story; as students mature and are able, allow them to make up the story.

Debriefing: Use the following questions to encourage discussion of the activity:
1. Did all of the storytellers continue to tell the same story?
2. Did the separate parts fit to make one continuous story, or did we make some turns?
3. Did some people hurry their turns? Or slow down so they could take more time?

Assessment: Observe students while they are listening. Consider students' posture, participation, and whether their part of the story makes sense in the context of the story that preceded it. Have students explain how their part fits the story if you do not see the connection. Question students regarding events or shifts in the story as the yarn changed color.

ACTIVITY

3.2   Invisible Speeches

Standard 13:   Competent listeners demonstrate knowledge and understanding of the listening process.

Grade Levels: 11–12

Description: This activity helps students focus on the nonverbal aspects of listening.

Objective: Students will demonstrate understanding of feedback, context, and shared responsibility in the listening process.

Materials: "The Invisible Speaker" evaluation form

Procedure:
1. Ask students to prepare a three- to five-minute informative and persuasive speech and present it to the class. The presentations should be read from prepared speeches, with the speaker invisible to the class but within earshot. Presenters may stand behind a screen or at the back of the room, but the class may not look at them during the presentation.

2. Instruct presenters to try to maintain the class's attention through the use of their voices alone. Do not allow any background music or sound effects.

3. Instruct listeners that they will be asked questions about the presentation.

4. As an alternative, have students listen to a famous speech (e.g., Martin Luther King, Jr.'s "I Have a Dream" or John F. Kennedy's inaugural address). Or, have them use an already prepared speech and work on delivering rather than on preparing the message.

Debriefing: Use the following questions to encourage discussion of the activity:

1. What was easy and what was difficult about giving this presentation?
2. How would you describe the speaker's voice?
3. What aspects of the presentation made listening easy?
4. What aspects of the presentation made listening difficult?
5. What elements of vocal skills should this speaker concentrate on to become more effective? Rate? Volume? Pause? Tone?
6. What can listeners do to be better listeners when they cannot see a speaker?

Assessment: Provide a brief written or oral critique to each student (see "The Invisible Speaker" evaluation form). Scripts of the speeches may also be turned in for evaluation.

Evaluation: The Invisible Speaker

Name: _____

Topic: _____

Speaker Qualities   *Listener Effects*

Volume: _____
_____

Articulation: _____
_____

Resonance: _____
_____

Pause: _____
_____

Rate: _____
_____

Pitch/Inflection: _____
_____

Tone of Voice: _____
_____

Energy/Enthusiasm: _____
_____

To what extent did the presentation hold the class's interest? Why?

_____
_____
_____
_____

ACTIVITY

3.3   The Listening Box

Standard 14: Competent listeners demonstrate the ability to use appropriate and effective listening skills for a given communication situation and setting.

Grade Levels: 7–8, 9–10

Description: This activity helps students to practice remembering information obtained through listening.

Objective: Students will demonstrate the principles of listening retention in an interpersonal communication context.

Materials: A large box with 20 to 30 personal items that illustrate personal information—for example, a picture of your pet, a videotape of your favorite movie, a poem that describes your life

Procedure:
1. Begin by telling the students that you want to share some personal information.
2. Then start by casually removing items from the box one at a time and discussing each item and its meaning.
3. During the course of the discussion, use the following to demonstrate the effect of using memory skills:

   Repetition: Discuss two objects more than once.

   Notetaking: Ask the class to write down a certain item and why it is important.

   Mnemonic Device: Create a mnemonic for a particular item and share that mnemonic with the class (e.g., "My favorite food is ice cream and ice cream starts with the same letters as the title of this class, Interpersonal Communication.").

   Focus Listener: Take one object and tell the class, "This is probably the most important item that describes me."

   Identify with the Audience: Choose one item that illustrates a characteristic you have in common with students in the class. For example, "This is one of my swimming medals. I still enjoy swimming, just like Tara, who is on the school swimming team."

Debriefing: Put everything back in the box. Ask students what objects they remember. Discuss which strategies you used to help students retain the information. Remind students of the strategies speakers can use to help listeners remember a message.

Assessment: Have students prepare listening boxes to share with classmates in small groups. After each presentation, class members should write down what objects they remembered and what techniques helped them to remember.

3.4   What I Hear You Saying Is . . .

Standard 14:   Competent listeners demonstrate the ability to use appropriate and effective listening skills for a given communication situation and setting.

Grade Levels: 7–8, 9–10 (depending on topics selected)

Description: This activity asks students to listen to discussion so that they can summarize not only the content but also the feelings behind messages.

Objective: Students will listen effectively to the content of messages and the feelings behind them.

Materials: None

Procedure: 1. Explain to students that speakers provide at least two types of information when they speak—content and feeling. Tell students that they will practice listening to both content and feeling in a message.

2. Place students in pairs, and offer the class a choice of three topics for discussion within each pair. Some possible topics for discussion are:

   • My favorite music

   • What I did during my vacation

   • What I like about my family

   • What I like best about using a computer

   • My favorite movie

   Possible topics also might be current events or other issues or ideas raised in content areas, for example, as part of a social studies lesson.

3. As discussion continues, periodically say, "Stop."

4. At these points, each student must repeat his or her partner's last statement in general terms in an attempt to summarize the message and the feeling of the statement. For example, "You were talking about your favorite computer game, called 'Spooks.' You felt good because you like to play the game because it makes you think."

5. Allow discussion to continue for 15 minutes or until interest wanes.

Debriefing: Ask the following questions to encourage discussion of the activity:

1. Was this challenging? How?

2. How often did listeners misinterpret what speakers were saying?

3. How did misinterpretation seem to occur?

4. How often did misinterpretation occur?

5. How did you feel (as a speaker) when you realized the listener was not listening or understanding?

6. How did you feel as a listener when you realized you had not listened?

7. Was it harder to hear content or feelings?

Assessment: Monitor students to determine that they are listening for the speaker's feelings, not for feelings described by the speaker. For example, "You were excited," not "You said your brother was excited." Students might evaluate each other and then evaluate themselves for accuracy. Listening for content and listening for feelings can be assessed separately.

ACTIVITY

3.5 | To Tell the Truth

Standard 14: Competent listeners demonstrate the ability to use appropriate and effective listening skills for a given communication situation and setting.

Grade Levels: 11–12

Description: This activity has students listen critically to political or product ads to determine what is being done to encourage people to vote for a candidate or buy a product.

Objective: Students will listen critically to advertisements.

Materials: Advertisements

Procedure:
1. Share political or product advertisements with the class. If this is a campaign year, political examples should be plentiful. If not, check with history or government teachers, who may have some examples stored away. You may also select product advertisements related to students' interests or levels, such as sports equipment or clothing.

2. Read the ads to the class, tape-record them from the radio, tape-record your own (with different voices and music), or video-record some from television. You might ask students to bring in examples from newspapers and magazines.

3. After experiencing each ad, ask each member of the class to write down (1) the main selling points of each commercial and (2) the differences between the products/candidates based on the information in the commercials.

Debriefing: Use the following questions to encourage discussion:

1. At what kind of audience was each commercial aimed? How did the advertiser slant the commercial to hit that audience?

2. Which ad was the most memorable? What do you remember of it? Why?

3. Which ad was the most persuasive? Why? Which ad had the most information?

4. Which commercial was most effective? Why?

5. Which ad seemed the most honest and the least manipulative?

6. What did the different ads stress? What did they downplay?

7. Is the most memorable and most persuasive ad the one that does the most to make you an informed voter/buyer?

8. What techniques have the advertisers used to make us listen?

9. What other techniques might the commercials have used to create the messages?

Assessment: Monitor students to determine which ones understand the relationships and have listened. A similar analysis of an advertisement might appear on an in-class test or an out-of-class essay assignment. Students might also be required to create their own advertisement designed to get others to really listen.

ACTIVITY

3.6 Talking Stick

Standard 15: Competent listeners demonstrate the ability to identify and manage barriers to listening.

Grade Levels: 9–10

Description: This small-group activity encourages students to practice listening when they would prefer to talk.

Objective: Students will recognize the effect of preconceived attitudes and biases, impatience, and other barriers to listening and will accept responsibility for managing barriers to listening.

Materials: A talking stick—this can be any stick, preferably a small tree branch, about 18 inches long. The stick can be decorated with a few strands of leather, some beads, and other small objects brought to class by students (e.g., feather, ribbon, small shells).

Procedure:
1. Have students sit in a circle. If preferable, divide the class into groups of six or seven students.
2. Instruct students that members can speak only when holding the stick and that no one is to interrupt the person who has the stick.
3. When a member is through speaking, the stick passes to the left and the speaker surrendering the stick must wait until it has made its way back around the circle before speaking again. This prevents the dialogue from becoming a contest of opposing positions and allows for "the long view," a perspective to which all others' perspectives have contributed.
4. Inform students about the three rules for the activity: speak honestly, be brief, and listen from the heart.
5. Encourage participants not to plan in advance what they are going to say but to wait until the stick is in their hands to discover what they want to contribute.
6. This activity may be conducted using a specific theme or topic, or the conversation may simply be opened to whatever participants feel moved to say. Some topics that work include school dress codes; overemphasis on sports in secondary schools; teenage drinking, smoking, or drug use; or a current events issue.

Debriefing: Use the following questions to encourage discussion of the activity:
1. How did it feel to have to wait your turn?
2. How much more did you get out of the topic from this method?
3. How did this method affect your mode of listening? Speaking?
4. How did the discussion flow differently than your normal discussion of a topic in class or with friends?
5. What biases or preconceived ways of thinking affected your listening?
6. What have you discovered about your attitude toward listening?
7. How can you practice these techniques in other listening situations?

Assessment: Observe students as they talk, and note differences from previous class discussions. Ask students to write a short paper in which they describe how this activity enhanced their listening skills. Ask students to summarize a part of the conversation or a specific member's contribution. Students could also be asked to paraphrase a segment of the conversation to practice this aspect of good listening.

ACTIVITY

3.7   May I Quote You?

Standard 15: Competent listeners demonstrate the ability to identify and manage barriers to listening.

Grade Levels: 11–12

Description: This activity helps students recognize their own biases and the effects of bias on the listening process.

Objective: Students will recognize the effects of various barriers on listening and summarize what someone else has said.

Materials: Appropriate quotations, "May I Quote You?" evaluation form

Procedure:
1. Select a series of quotations appropriate to the subject matter and grade level of students. The following quotations might be used:
   - "I disapprove of what you say, but I will defend to the death your right to say it." —Voltaire
   - "Nothing so needs reforming as other people's habits." —Mark Twain
   - "Nature has given to man one tongue, but two ears, that we hear from others twice as much as we speak." —Epictetus
2. Present a quotation to the class.
3. Assign students to work in pairs; the students in a pair will be designated Student A and Student B.
4. Ask the students to use the following procedure in response to the quotations.
   - Student A states her idea about the quotation, without interruption from Student B.
   - Student B summarizes what Student A said.
   - Student B states his beliefs.
   - Student A summarizes Student B's position.

Debriefing: Use the following questions to encourage discussion of the activity:
1. Did your own ideas about the quotation inhibit your ability to listen and, as a result, to summarize another's views accurately?
2. What might you do to remedy this situation?
3. Did you want to interrupt?
4. Why is it important to be able to summarize accurately what another person tells us?
5. How does this affect the communication process?
6. Can you think of situations in which you summarized another message incorrectly (for example, a teacher's, friend's, parent's, or sibling's message) and the incorrect summation led to communication problems? Describe the situation.

Assessment: Give students the "May I Quote You?" evaluation form to evaluate their partners according to the criteria presented.

Evaluation: "May I Quote You?"

My Name:

_____

My Partner's Name:

_____

My position was:

_____

_____

_____

My partner summarized my position as:

_____

_____

_____

My partner (accurately/inaccurately) summarized my position:

_____

My partner was courteous even when our positions were in conflict.

Yes _____ No _____

I felt my partner was interested in what I had to say.

Yes _____ No _____

MEDIA LITERACY

TEACHING ACTIVITIES FOR NCA STANDARDS 16-20

Introduction

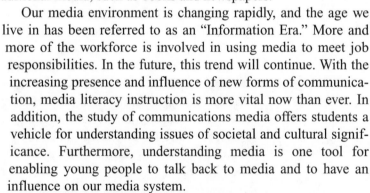

The many and varied forms of media play an important role in our everyday lives. It is amazing to think that electronic media, which are so pervasive and integral to our daily lives, have appeared only in the last century. Life without film, radio, television, and computers is difficult to imagine for many adults and for most children. Whether we use them for entertainment, for work, to relieve boredom, or to find information, electronic media are as much a part of our lives as more traditional media, such as books and newspapers.

Our media environment is changing rapidly, and the age we live in has been referred to as an "Information Era." More and more of the workforce is involved in using media to meet job responsibilities. In the future, this trend will continue. With the increasing presence and influence of new forms of communication, media literacy instruction is more vital now than ever. In addition, the study of communications media offers students a vehicle for understanding issues of societal and cultural significance. Furthermore, understanding media is one tool for enabling young people to talk back to media and to have an influence on our media system.

Communication using media involves the creation of a message by a person or group that is communicated via a specific medium to an audience. In essence, the communication process includes (1) a sender (the message creator), (2) the channel (radio, television, film, Internet, newspaper, magazine, etc.), (3) a receiver (the audience), (4) the message (images, sounds, words, etc.), and (5) feedback (responses or reactions from the receiver to the sender).

Media literacy is the ability to access, analyze, evaluate, and produce media messages in various forms. Our relationship to the media we consume is quite complicated. Our media experiences are both personal and public. Each person interprets and uses media differently. However, media producers or message senders use specific conventions and methods to gain attention. Because media messages are created by people, all

73

messages have a point of view that can be identified through careful analysis of language or image use. Messages are not value free. Understanding how the message creator influences the meaning and content of the message is the first step toward media literacy.

The second step toward media literacy involves the process of interpretation. Although message creators expect receivers to interpret messages in the same way they are intended, we know this is not always the case. People will always interpret messages uniquely. Nonetheless, as educators we can teach our students how to approach a media text, the processes involved in the creation of various kinds of media, and perhaps most important, what questions to ask while interpreting the message.

The teaching activities in this unit are designed to help students define media, lead them toward an understanding of how they and others use media, and provide insight into the complexity of relationships among audiences and media content. In addition, they are geared toward helping students understand that social and cultural contexts produce the specific content of media and that media use occurs within social contexts. Since most of our media content is commercially produced, activities directed toward understanding the commercial nature of media are included. The goal is to build awareness of the influences and strategies directed toward generating revenue through the commercial media system. The five standards for media literacy (see Figure I.1) were designed to help students learn about the role and impact of media in their various forms on their lives. The final standard ensures that students also gain experience in producing their own media content so that they will know how to use media to communicate with specific audiences.

To fully appreciate the complex nature of various media and how we use them, we need to talk about media in relationship to other areas of study. Research reveals that students enjoy class more when the teacher uses examples from the media. In addition, students are able to relate to subject matter more intimately when it reflects their everyday experiences. Media education is fun and interesting for students while providing them with specific cognitive and critical thinking skills.

Media education is a student-centered approach to teaching that provides many opportunities for students to constructively develop their own voice or point of view. At the same time, it provides structure for analysis and evaluation. Assessments for many of the high school activities are writing assignments, presentations, or group projects. Therefore, student reactions to various media products should not be graded as right or wrong; they are more or less supported or informed. Student opinions and reactions need to be based on evidence from the specific media texts used in class or for homework. A rubric for evaluating student work should include how well students support their interpretations, identify visual and auditory details, and apply critical thinking to their analyses.

4.1   My Daily Media

Standard 16: Media-literate communicators demonstrate knowledge and understanding of the ways people use media in their personal and public lives.

Grade Levels: 9–10, 11–12

Description: In this activity, students keep track of their media use and consumption patterns, allowing for reflection on their media consumption habits.

Objective: Students will develop an awareness of their media consumption patterns and use.

Materials: Writing utensils, "My Daily Media Log" worksheet, a media log (composition notebook) or paper

Procedure:
1. Discuss with students the emotional and psychological reasons for consuming different media. How we communicate with others and the media we consume reveal a lot about who we are and what we like. Researchers claim that the average U. S. citizen is in contact with some form of electronic media for 35 or more hours per week. Considering the time most people spend consuming media, it stands to reason we should understand how, why, when, what, and with whom it is used. When we consciously consume media, we are more likely to critically examine what we see, hear, and read.

2. Ask students to respond to the following questions in writing and verbally:
   a. What are the electronic media you use most frequently (television, videogames, radio, etc.)?
   b. Why do you use each medium (relaxation, boredom, schoolwork, for fun, to find information, entertainment, etc.)?
   c. With whom do you usually use each medium you've listed (parents, friends, siblings, alone)?
   d. At what times do you usually use each medium (after school, in the morning, after school, during school, before bed)?
   e. For how long do you use each medium (1 hour, 30 minutes, 10 minutes, etc.)?

3. After students have identified what, when, and with whom they most commonly consume media, assign homework in which they must keep track of specific media use. Over the course of a typical week, have students record their media use and consumption patterns using the "My Daily Media Log" worksheet. The purpose of the exercise is for students to notice actual use and reflect upon their media consumption habits.

Debriefing: Encourage students to discuss what they have discovered about their media use; point to differences between in-class recollections and out-of-class observations. Chart before-and-after usage patterns on the chalkboard.

Assessment: In writing, have students identify how, why, when, and with whom they use specific media. Have them respond to the following questions:

1. Are there certain rules for media use at home? Can you watch whenever and whatever you'd like? Can you connect to the Internet without restriction?

2. Who has control of the television remote? What media do you have in your bedroom?

3. Is using media alone different from using it with others? How?

4. Do you perform other tasks while consuming media (e.g., homework with the TV)? What activities do you do simultaneously?

5. What feelings do you experience after consuming each medium (e.g., guilty, tired, sad, happy, angry, bored)? Why? Do your feelings differ depending on the medium?

Students should discuss the different cognitive and affective states they experience before and after consumption of various media. Consider alternatives to media consumption and strategies for ongoing critical awareness of media use behaviors. As part of the assessment, have students consider how media consumption changes when with another person and how watching critically changes the viewing, listening, and reading experience.

My Daily Media Log

Throughout a typical day, most of us consume a variety of media. From the moment we wake in the morning to the moment we fall asleep at night, we are exposed to or engage with one medium or another. Fill in each medium (television, radio, books, etc.) you use, including the time of day (exact times), the content (what are you listening to, reading, watching, etc.), the length of time spent with the medium (5 minutes, 1 hour, 5 hours, etc.), why you are using it (bored, background sound, research, relaxation, etc.), and who you are with (alone, parents, friends, siblings, etc.). Use one or more pages per day.

Day of Week _____

Medium:	Medium:	Medium:
Content:	Content:	Content:
Time of Day:	Time of Day:	Time of Day:
Length of time:	Length of time:	Length of time:
Why are you using the medium?	Why are you using the medium?	Why are you using the medium?
Who are you with?	Who are you with?	Who are you with?

Medium:	Medium:	Medium:
Content:	Content:	Content:
Time of Day:	Time of Day:	Time of Day:
Length of time:	Length of time:	Length of time:
Why are you using the medium?	Why are you using the medium?	Why are you using the medium?
Who are you with?	Who are you with?	Who are you with?

4.2 Defining Media Channels

Standard 16: Media-literate communicators demonstrate knowledge and understanding of the ways people use media in their personal and public lives.

Grade Levels: 9–10, 11–12

Description: The first steps in understanding our media use are to identify and define the channels of communication we use most frequently and why. Before students can fully appreciate the diversity of each medium, they need to identify and differentiate the qualities associated with each. Although one medium is not better than another, each medium is more or less appropriate for certain contexts and messages. Media channels are one part of the communication process that includes the following basic components: a sender, a receiver, the channel, and the message.

Objective: Students will identify the primary characteristics of various media and explain why they prefer specific media.

Materials: Writing utensils, "Media Characteristics" worksheet, blank paper, or a composition notebook

Procedure:
1. Explain to students that the process of communication at a minimum includes a sender, a receiver, a channel, a message, and feedback. The first steps in understanding our media use is to define and identify the channels of communication we use most frequently and why. Before students can fully appreciate the diversity of each medium, they need to identify and differentiate the qualities associated with each. Although one medium is not better than another, each medium is more or less appropriate for certain contexts and messages.

2. Discuss the concept of media channels with the class. Channels of communication include such media as telephone, television, magazines, newspapers, broadcast news, e-mail, videogames, and movies.

3. Have students identify and list channels of communication they regularly use.

4. Based on the list, brainstorm with students the characteristics of each medium. To assist with identifying characteristics, consider the following questions:
   a. Is it print or nonprint?
   b. Is it a visual medium?
   c. Does it use sound?
   d. Does it allow interactive communication or only one-way communication?
   e. Is it a mass medium? How many senders to how many receivers?
   f. Is it expensive? Convenient? Who has access?

5. Encourage students to develop additional distinguishing characteristics.

Debriefing: Urge students to capture in writing what they have identified, using the "Media Characteristics" worksheet. Media logs promote writing as well as provide documentation for students to return to as they reflect on their media use over a period of time. As homework or an in-class writing assignment, ask students to respond to the following questions or statements in their media journals:

1. Identify the media you use most frequently.

2. Rank your media preferences (television programs, videogames, radio stations, films, etc.) starting with 1.

3. Explain why you prefer certain media to others.

4. What are the strengths and weaknesses of your preferred media?

Assessment: Ask students to identify the components of the communication process, define the term "media," generate a list of media, and identify the characteristics of each medium. In addition, have students identify media they prefer and explain why, referring back to the qualities of each medium that make it unique.

Media Characteristics

Each medium has various characteristics that make it unique. In order to recognize the differences, we need to identify them. Fill in the appropriate characteristics (across the top) for the medium (column to left) in the empty boxes. Blank columns and rows are available for additional information.

	Text, images, and/or sound	Moving or still images	Sound types (voices, music)	Interactive or one-way	# of senders to # of receivers	Cost	Who has access	Ease of use		
Television										
Radio										
Film										
Magazines										
Books										
Videogames										
Computer w/ Internet connection										
Computer w/o Internet connection										
DVD player										
Newspaper										
Telephone										

Definitions and Terms

Media Characteristics Grid

Text, images, and/or sounds: Write down which techniques the medium uses to create meaning. In this activity, text is considered written language. Images include moving and still pictures.

Moving or still images: Write down the type of images used. Moving images are similar to what is seen in film or television. Still images are used in magazines and newspapers, for example.

Sound types: Indicate which types of sounds are used to create meaning. Consider voices, music, singing, bleeps, crashes, and so forth. Some media do not use sound.

Interactive or one-way: Consider whether you have the ability to communicate with the sender. An interactive medium allows simultaneous communication (e.g., the telephone). One-way communication means you cannot provide immediate feedback to the source or sender (e.g., television). Write down your responses.

Number of senders to number of receivers: Consider who is sending and receiving the message. Write down the number of senders to the number of receivers (e.g., television programming: one sender to millions of receivers).

Cost: How much money does the medium require for use? In addition to purchasing the medium, consider whether you have to pay a fee for access or use (e.g., computer with Internet connection). Write down your response.

Access: Consider who has access to the medium. Can everyone receive, use, or purchase the medium? Write down who does not have access.

Ease of use: On a scale of 1 to 5, rate how easy (1) or difficult (5) the medium is to use.

ACTIVITY

| 4.3 | **Media Characters and Real People** |

Standard 17: Media-literate communicators demonstrate knowledge and understanding of the complex relationships among audiences and media content.

Grade Levels: 7–8

Description: This activity encourages students to think about how people and life in the United States are represented on television and in movies. It raises the issue of stereotypes, allowing older students to begin to question media representations and images with regard to various stereotypes. They will learn to read physical and behavioral cues (clothing, hairstyles, interactive styles) to interpret characterizations.

Objective: Students will recognize the difference between the fictional world of TV and movies and the real world.

Materials: Writing materials; television monitor optional

Procedure:
1. Pose the following scenario and questions to students:

   Some students from another country are planning a visit to our city or town. These students have never been to the United States before and have decided to try to learn what they can through watching American television and movies. What might surprise them about our town if they are expecting it to be like the movies and TV?

   Show a sampling of television content by channel surfing and spending several seconds on each channel, to help students think about questions involving stereotypes. The channel surfing tape should be made at a time when students are likely to be viewing—for example, right after school or in the evening.

2. List the students' impressions on the chalkboard as they respond to the following questions:

   a. Do you think they will get an accurate picture of what our town and people are like?

   b. What might surprise them about our town if they are expecting it to be like the movies and TV?

   c. What will they expect in terms of our quality of life? Rich, poor, or in between?

   d. What will they think about the way we look and dress?

   e. What will they expect our houses to be like?

   f. Do you think they will expect to find a lot of crime and violence?

   g. What will they think about how women and girls behave? Boys and men? People of different races and ethnic groups (stereotypes)?

   h. What will they think of how we solve problems?

   i. What will they think of the kind of humor we have and the jokes we make?

   j. Will they think we are polite or rude?

   k. What will they think about any extraordinary powers we might have?

Debriefing: Point out to the students the discrepancies between what they thought the visitor would expect based on media images and representations and what they think their town and its people are really like. Raise the question of whether these media characterizations might affect the way they think about themselves and their own lives in comparison to what they see through media.

Assessment: Have students report on differences between real-life people and situations and those reflected through media. Ask them for explanations concerning the differences between media people and situations and real people and situations. Ask students to define and give examples of stereotypes. Develop a chart on the chalkboard divided into the categories of "TV" and "Reality." Have students generate ideas for characteristics and categorize them, noting which ones represent stereotypes.

ACTIVITY

4.4   Millions of Magazines

Standard 17: Media-literate communicators demonstrate knowledge and understanding of the complex relationships among audiences and media content.

Grade Levels: 9–10

Description: In this exercise, students closely analyze popular fashion magazines for explicit and implicit ideology, as reflected in the language and images used.

Objective: Students will evaluate media content for explicit and implicit ideology as expressed in the pictures, words, and images of popular magazines.

Materials: A variety of popular fashion magazines, "Millions of Magazines" worksheet

Procedure: Magazines have a long and rich history in the United States. Benjamin Franklin's publication in 1741, *The General Magazine and Historical Chronicles for all the British Plantations in America,* is credited as the first U. S. magazine. Although the look and content of magazines have evolved over time, the values and ideologies that are inherently part of all magazine publications are still evident. Today, hundreds of different magazines are published and are read by millions of people. Magazines reflect the diversity and complexity of audience needs and interests.

Assign students to small groups, provide copies of popular magazines, and ask each group to respond to the following questions for each magazine:

1. To whom does the magazine appeal?
2. What or who is on the front cover? What does the cover indicate about the content?
3. What definitions of happiness, success, beauty, and power are implied in the pictures, advertisements, and editorials?
4. Are any groups excluded from the pictures or articles? Whom? Why?
5. What types of stories or feature articles are present? Whose point of view do they represent?
6. Are there differences in gender, class, and race representations? How is each portrayed?
7. What values, beliefs, and ideologies are implied?
8. Who would be most interested in this magazine? Who would be least interested? Why?

Debriefing: Values, beliefs, and assumptions about the world are implied through images and language. Encourage students to consider how media content reflects the assumed interests of specific groups. What would a nonnative citizen assume about U. S. culture based on the images found within our popular fashion magazines?

Assessment: Assign students a magazine (architectural, fashion, news, cooking, animal, dirt bike racing, videogames, etc.) to review individually. Ask students to respond to the questions on the "Millions of Magazines" worksheet. As a group, compare and contrast the various magazines. Looking at the table of contents, the advertisements, and the stories, identify and discuss the similarities and differences among them. How does the content change depending on the magazine? What beliefs, values, and ideologies are embedded in the content (language, images, narrative, and design) of each magazine? What is important to the reader of the selected magazine? How do you know? Who is excluded? Students should consider how and why they prefer certain magazines to others. Grading should be based on sophistication of analysis and response.

Millions of Magazines

To develop a deeper appreciation and understanding of the relationship between audiences and media content, you need to know what questions and issues to consider. This activity provides a starting place for many topics and issues involved in magazine publishing, such as content, layout, design, audience appeal, and point of view.

Directions: Using a magazine assigned to you, respond to each of the following statements or questions.

What is the magazine title and date of circulation?

_____

_____

Where can the magazine be purchased?

_____

_____

Who or what appears on the front cover?

_____

_____

What does the magazine cover reveal about the content?

_____

_____

What is the cost of the magazine?

_____

_____

What is the genre of the magazine (fashion, sports, news, etc.)?

_____

_____

Look at the table of contents. What does it reveal about the content?

_____

_____

(continued)

Millions of Magazines *continued*

How many pages does the magazine contain? What percentage of the magazine is dedicated to advertisements? What percentage is dedicated to articles?

_____

_____

Is there any relationship between the advertisements and the articles? What is the relationship? (Do any articles support or identify any products and services offered in the magazine?)

_____

_____

What and how are colors used to attract attention?

_____

_____

What products and services are advertised?

_____

_____

What assumptions does the magazine make about its readers?

_____

_____

Who is the target audience? (Support your response with specific examples from the text.)

_____

_____

Would you read this magazine? Why? Why not?

_____

_____

Do you read any specific magazines? Name them. Why do you like the magazines you have named?

_____

_____

Do you think a magazine with broad audience appeal would be successful? Why or why not?

_____

_____

4.5   Target Audience

Standard 17: Media-literate communicators demonstrate knowledge and understanding of the complex relationships among audiences and media content.

Grade Levels: 11–12

Description: In this activity, students view commercials and use related demographic information to explore the concept of target audience.

Objective: Students will understand and identify the relationship between products/services and television program content by conducting content analyses.

Materials: Pencil and paper, VCR or DVD, TV, various recorded television advertisements, "Target Audience Content Analysis" worksheets

Procedure: All media messages are developed with particular audiences in mind. Public speakers and mass media producers develop messages to attract the attention of specific audiences. Within a mass media context, the target audience is the group of people an advertiser wants to influence. The following types of information reflect demographic data: age, gender, marital status, physical condition, occupation, level of education, place of residence, ethnicity, profession, and so forth. Television programs are created to appeal to various demographic groups so that advertisers can reach specific target audiences.

1. Ask students to identify their favorite television programs. Explain to students that different programs attract different groups of viewers. Because of this, advertisers air specific commercials during particular programs to ensure they reach the desired target audience. Advertisers know what programs are viewed, when, and by whom.

2. In class, show commercials from Saturday morning (8 to 10 A.M.) and one weekday evening night (8 to 10 P.M.). Tell students when each commercial aired.

3. After viewing, ask students to respond to the questions on the in-class "Target Audience Content Analysis" worksheet.

Debriefing: Discuss the similarities and differences between the television program and the commercials, referring to specific visual and auditory cues in each media text. What is the relationship between the advertised products and the program content? What do the images reveal to you about the target audience? Is this an accurate portrayal of the demographic group? Why or why not?

Assessment: As homework, have students respond to the questions on the take-home "Target Audience Content Analysis" worksheet. Ask students to conduct a content analysis of their favorite television program. Students may want to or be required to videotape their program for future analyses. As they view, students should record how many commercials aired, the products and/or services most commonly shown (fast food, clothing, etc.), and the characteristics of the people depicted in the advertisements. They should also identify the television program's name; the date and time of airing; the gender, ages, and professions of the main characters; the setting of the program; and any other relevant information. The assignment should be graded based on students' sophistication of analysis.

Target Audience Content Analysis

(In-Class Activity)

Television Program _____   Time and Day _____

Product or Service Advertised _____

How many people or characters are in the advertisement? _____

Physically describe the people or characters in the advertisement (age, gender, profession, economic status, ethnicity, etc.).

_____

_____

Why do you think the advertiser made the decision to include those specific types of people?

_____

_____

What type of music is used, if any? Why do you think it was selected?

_____

_____

What is the setting or context of the advertisement (kitchen, office, garden, etc.)? How does the setting relate to the product?

_____

_____

Identify the television program's main characters, setting, and primary narrative. To whom do these appeal most?

_____

_____

How does the television program's theme and ideology support or contradict the product or service? Give specific examples.

_____

_____

After closely examining the advertisement's content, what have you learned about the intended target audience?

_____

_____

Target Audience Content Analysis

(Take-Home Activity)

For this activity, you will select and view your favorite television program. If you do not have a favorite, select one you would like to watch. You may consider using a television schedule for suggestions. You may want to record your program for future analyses. You will need to keep track of the number and kinds of advertisements aired during the program you selected. Keep this form with you as you view so you can write down specific details as they occur.

Name of program: _____

Time and date of program: _____

Main characters (gender, age, social status, occupation, etc.):

_____

_____

Theme or story line of program:

_____

_____

Location or setting:

_____

_____

How many commercials aired during the program? _____

What products and/or services were advertised? List each.

_____

_____

Based on the information you have observed, identify the target audience. Explain your choice. Support your opinion with specific information from the program and the advertisements.

_____

_____

Do you think the representation of people in the advertisements and the commercials are stereotypical? Why or why not?

_____

_____

A C T I V I T Y

4.6   A Peek Behind the Scenes

Standard 18: Media-literate communicators demonstrate knowledge and understanding that media content is produced within social and cultural contexts.

Grade Levels: 7–8

Description: This activity teaches students how media content is produced through direct contact with a media production facility or media professional.

Objective: Students will understand that media content is constructed and that a variety of media professionals participate in that process.

Materials: Writing materials, videotape of credits of selected media productions, "A Peek Behind the Scenes" worksheet

Procedure:

1. Ask students to think about who creates programs and other media content.

2. Run the credits for a movie or television program that is geared to the students' age-group, such as the credits for a situation comedy or a news program. Have them complete the "A Peek Behind the Scenes" worksheet after they view the video.

3. Have students create a list of questions they have about how content is produced.

4. Plan a field trip to a media facility—for instance, a local TV station, radio station, or newspaper. If that is not possible, invite a local celebrity or media professional to the school. Ask the professional to talk about her job so that students will know that many people are behind the scenes in media facilities. Ask her to talk with the students about the differences between locally produced content and content that comes from other places (network, syndication, etc.).

5. Have the students investigate the following media production roles and terms:

   Director—supervises the flow of the actual content

   Producer—plans and coordinates all elements needed for a program; sometimes plays a role in financing a product

   Writer—writes the script

   Talent—actors and others who appear on air in the finished product

   Camera operator—responsible for running the camera

   Audio operator—arranges microphones and makes sure all sounds are at the proper levels

   Floor personnel—responsible for making sure all activities in the studio proceed as planned; in television, they act as facilitators for communications between director and actors

   Lighting engineer—responsible for arranging for appropriate lighting

   Makeup—responsible for talents' makeup

   Wardrobe—responsible for talents' dress/costumes

   Script/Continuity—in film, makes sure that all shots are noted and that all details in shots remain consistent for editing

Editor—responsible for taking raw footage and linking it in a logical, artistic way to tell the story

Props—items on the set used to create the impression needed for a scene

Cartoonist—responsible for drawing people, animals, events, and situations

Debriefing: As a follow-up to the visit, involve students in a discussion of what surprised them or interested them most about how local media work and the jobs involved in providing programs and other content. Ask students to think about the aspect of media production that interests them most, and have them create a picture or collage to illustrate that aspect.

Assessment: Have students identify the different jobs that go into creating and distributing media content and some of the equipment necessary to produce content. Have students go to the library or search online to research a media professional role that is of interest to them. Have them work in teams and present results to the class in oral or written form.

A Peek Behind the Scenes

Match the term to its definition.

_____ Director   A. Writes the script

_____ Writer   B. Actors and others who are on air

_____ Talent   C. Responsible for dress and costumes

_____ Wardrobe   D. Observes and supervises all aspects of a show's creation

_____ Editor   E. Responsible for linking original video

_____ Producer   F. Plans all activities related to the TV program, movie, or advertisement

Who helped create this message?

Your teacher will show you a short video clip from a film, a television program, an advertisement, or a cartoon. After you view it, answer the questions.

What type of program is it? (Circle your answer)

Movie   Cartoon   TV program   Advertisement

Check the box next to the name of the person who helped create the message.

Helped	Did Not Help	People Who Helped Make the Movie, Cartoon, TV Program, or Advertisement
☐	☐	Director
☐	☐	Producer
☐	☐	Actor
☐	☐	Cartoonist
☐	☐	Editor
☐	☐	Lighting Engineer
☐	☐	Camera Operator
☐	☐	Audio Operator

ACTIVITY

4.7   As Time Goes By

Standard 18:   Media-literate communicators demonstrate knowledge and understanding that media content is produced within social and cultural contexts.

Grade Levels: 9–10, 11–12

Description: In this activity, students compare the ways social issues were presented in film in the past to how they are presented today.

Objective: Students will identify how a specific social phenomenon changes over time.

Materials: VCR, selected films or video-recorded television programs, writing utensils

Procedure:
1. Discuss with students how media products reflect the values, beliefs, and ideologies of specific social and cultural contexts. The specific subject matter can be related to any one of a variety of social topics, including marriage, family, work, leadership, attitudes toward war, and so forth. The purpose of the activity is to encourage students to identify how media content usually reflects the dominant ideology of the society in which it is produced.

2. Ask students to consider how relationships, courting, and dating have changed over the past 50 years.

3. Generate a list of the differences and similarities.

4. Select and show a popular film from the 1940s or 1950s. If possible, select a film that has been remade recently, such as *Father of the Bride.* If it is not possible to use a film, consider showing an older television program, such as *Father Knows Best* or *My Three Sons,* and compare it to *Friends* or *Will & Grace.* Show students various scenes of the original version in class.

5. As students view the films or television programs, have them consider the following questions (other questions will depend on other learning objectives):

    a. How do individuals communicate most frequently (phone, mail, etc.)?

    b. How is marriage portrayed?

    c. How is friendship represented? How do friends act toward one another?

    d. What kind of language is used? Are the words similar to or different from words used today?

    e. How do the characters behave toward one another?

    f. How is intimacy suggested (hugging, holding hands, etc.)?

    g. What type of conflict or concerns do the characters need to resolve?

    h. Are there any product placements?

    i. Is this a realistic portrayal of the society? Why or why not?

Debriefing: As homework, have students select a film or television program from a preapproved list. The film or television program should have been produced within the past few years. If at all possible, students should view the most recent version of the film or program. Have students answer the following questions to compare and contrast the old and new media product (questions will depend on learning objectives of related classroom materials):

1. How do the main characters communicate most frequently?

2. How are men and women portrayed in each? What are their responsibilities?

3. What style of clothes do they wear? Are they the same as or different from the older media text? How are they different and similar?

4. What is the biggest problem, concern, or issue confronting the main characters? Are the concerns the same or different?

5. How are marriage and family represented?

6. What artistic and visual differences are evident in the production of each?

7. How many product placements did you notice?

8. Which one is a more accurate representation of the society in which it was produced? Why? How do you know?

Many questions will depend on the specific films selected for analysis.

Assessment: Students should share their reactions to each film or program in writing and verbally. By comparing and contrasting various elements and characteristics of each program, students should relate their observations to the social expectations of the culture at the time the film or program was produced. Arguments must be supported with specific evidence from the program or film. Internet or library research may be needed for more sophisticated analysis and understanding of the time period in which the media product was produced.

ACTIVITY

4.8   Rock-n-Listen

Standard 18:   Media-literate communicators demonstrate knowledge and understanding that media content is produced within social and cultural contexts.

Grade Levels: 9–10, 11–12

Description: In this activity, students listen to selections from a variety of music genres to develop an understanding of how music both shapes and reflects ways of seeing the world.

Objective: Students will understand how different styles of music shape and reflect the point of view of specific cultural contexts.

Materials: Audiocassette or CD player, songs from a variety of music genres

Procedure: Music plays an important role in the development of youth culture. Many students identify with specific music groups and singers because music explores emotions and feelings in ways that are common to the listening audience. Audience issues of identity are intimately related to the mood, tone, lyrics, and presentation of the artist(s) and are evident in the conventions and content of each genre.

1. Discuss with students how music shapes and reflects ways of seeing the world. In class, play various genres of music, including rap, country, hard rock, jazz, world music, pop rock, classic rock, and so forth. Ask students to identify each song's genre. Encourage students to identify and share their responses.

2. After listening, hand out the lyrics to two or three of the songs played. Read the lyrics of the songs out loud with the class.

3. Ask students to identify the themes in each song by circling key words or phrases. Discuss findings with the class.

4. As a class, consider how the lyrics represent the genre and societal expectations. Can the students support their opinions with evidence from the lyrics?

5. Discuss various conventions of music. Ask the following questions:

    a. How fast is the beat?

    b. What types of instruments are used (drums, guitar, piano, violin, etc.)?

    c. How do you feel after listening (happy, sad, excited, scared, etc.)?

    d. How is language used to express emotion? Are the words positive or negative?

    e. What are the themes of each song (relationships, love, friendship, traveling, drinking, war, etc.)?

Debriefing: Encourage students to discuss the various characteristics of each genre. Open discussion is an important part of the learning experience. Students will hear various points of view and interpretations. Have students identify the differences and similarities among various genres of music by categorizing selected songs into different themes (content) as well as lyrical sounds (conventions). Students should respond to how music affects emotions as well as sense of identity.

Assessment: As homework, have students interview their parents or caregivers about their favorite music group, musician, or singer from their youth. As part of the assignment, students can submit the questions they asked as well as the responses they received. After the interview, instruct students to select one song identified by the caregiver and one personal favorite for analysis. A remix or remake of a song may also be used. Assessment is based on students' ability to:

1. Identify their caregiver's favorite song and musical group

2. Identify a personal favorite song and musical group

3. Analyze song lyrics for specific thematic issues

4. Identify key words and phrases in each (If not familiar with places or names, students need to identify the relevance of language to the overall meaning. This may require research.)

5. Explain how the themes of each song reflect the social concerns and issues of the era during which it was created

6. Categorize each song into a genre and explain why the genre was selected

7. Provide support of classification based on the content and conventions of the song

8. Respond to whether or not the musical group can be viewed on MTV or VH1 and explain what role, if any, music videos play in the "listening" experience of both selections

9. Consider what thoughts and/or emotions are evoked after listening

10. Compare and contrast both songs in terms of beat, lyrics, use of instruments, emotional affect, and intended audience

11. Respond to the differences and similarities between the themes of both songs (Specific reasons need to be identified and discussed.)

As a presentation and writing assignment, students should have the opportunity to share their perspective verbally and in writing. Student analysis must be supported with specific information from the song's content and the parent/caregiver interviews.

ACTIVITY

4.9   Advertising's Appeal

Standard 19: Media-literate communicators demonstrate knowledge and understanding of the commercial nature of media.

Grade Levels: 7–8

Description: This activity provides students, through the analysis of various ads, with the tools to identify and analyze the appeal of advertising.

Objective: Students will recognize ads, learn that commercial media are funded by advertising, and identify certain appeals that are used in advertising to elicit emotional responses from audience members.

Materials: Samples of ads that target various audiences (children, teens, and adults). These can be print, audio, video, and/or interactive. Choose from or combine art materials, print materials, audio recorder, video camera, and video playback equipment.

Procedure: 1. Raise the question of how commercial media production is funded. Point out to students that advertising is a major source of that funding.

2. Provide examples of print, television, radio, and Internet advertising to illustrate the various looks and appeals of advertising and the techniques that are used to create the desire to buy items.

3. Ask students if they have ever bought—or requested that someone buy them—a product based on how it looked or sounded in an ad. Were they ever disappointed that the product was not what they thought it would be? Lead students in a class discussion of these experiences.

4. Raise the question of how one can tell if something is advertising. Emphasize the persuasive nature of advertising.

5. Give examples of advertising content that is merged with narrative content (advertorials, character-based programs, Web pages, etc.) and have them break down which aspects have a selling intent and which do not. Introduce students to the idea of "target audience" advertisements—that is, advertising that is developed with particular audiences in mind as consumers of products.

6. For each ad, ask students who they think is the intended audience and how they can tell.

7. Raise the issue of whether the product is something that the audience really needs or whether it is something a person would not need but might want. Advertising creates desire for products in many ways. Several appeals are listed below. You may be able to identify others with the students. For starters, provide examples and describe the following advertising appeals:

    a. Image—Buy this product and you will be cool like the people in the ad.

    b. Bandwagon—Everyone is using this product; you should too if you want to be like everyone else.

    c. Testimonial—A famous person endorses this product, so you should buy it.

    d. Plain folks—Regular people use and like this product, so it is for you.

e. Name calling—The competing product is not up to par; you should buy our product.

f. Weasel—Makes a claim that is not really supported or promised, such as "this product may help under certain conditions."

g. Fun—Using this product makes your life more fun; buy it and enjoy life more.

h. Romance—Owning this product will make someone love you more.

Debriefing: Assign students, working in a medium of choice, alone or in groups, to invent or select a product for a target audience and plan an advertisement for that product (including such elements as script, storyboard, and/or plans for print layout). Have them employ some of the appeals introduced in class.

Assessment: Students should present their product and advertising appeal in class. Students should know that our commercial media system is funded largely through advertising. Show students various types of content and advertising materials and ask them to differentiate advertising from other content. Students should recognize when advertising and other content are merged. They should know that advertising is designed to create memory about and desires for products. Have students identify and define advertising appeals.

ACTIVITY

4.10   Look at Me—I'm Better and Faster!

Standard 19: Media-literate communicators demonstrate knowledge and understanding of the commercial nature of media.

Grade Levels: 9–10

Description: In this activity, students learn 10 advertising examples and locate examples of each.

Objective: Students will be able to list, define, and identify 10 different techniques used by advertisers.

Materials: Examples of each type of advertisement in print, audio, or video form

Procedure: Advertising uses various techniques to gain and attract attention. In order to critically analyze advertisements, it is vital to understand the various ways advertisers attempt to gain our attention. The following techniques are 10 of the most common advertising strategies. Discuss each of the 10 techniques with students, using specific examples from television, magazines, and radio. List the terms and definitions on the board for discussion.

1. *The Unfinished Claim:* The ad claims the product is better or has something more, but it does not finish its claim. Example: "Misty gives you more." (More what?)

2. *Glittering Generality:* The ad uses common words to describe the product. Example: *helps, virtually, like, works, fights, tastes, strong, can be, refreshes, clean.*

3. *"We Are Different and Unique" Claim:* The ad implies that the product is superior because it is different and/or unique. Example: "There's no other car like it."

4. *"Rain Is Wet" Claim:* The ad states something that is true for any brand in the product category. Example: "ROXY—the detergent gasoline" (true of any gasoline).

5. *"So What" Claim:* The ad states something that is true but that is not an advantage of the product. Example: "Strong enough for a man, but made for a woman."

6. *Vague Claim:* Colorful but meaningless words are used to create a category that overlaps with others. Example: "Lips have never looked so kissable." (Can this be proved?)

7. *Testimonial or Endorsement:* A celebrity appears in an ad to lend his or her star qualities to the product. Example: Michael Jordan endorsing sneakers.

8. *Scientific or Statistical Claim:* The ad refers to impressive-sounding numbers that are meaningless. Example: "Nine out of ten moms prefer 'X' for tough stains." (Where did this information come from?)

9. *"You're So Smart!" Claim:* The ad compliments consumers by making them feel special, important, and/or intelligent for selecting the product. Example: "You've come a long way, baby."

10. *Rhetorical Question:* The ad raises a question that demands a positive audience response that affirms the product. Example: "Wouldn't you rather have a Buick?"

Debriefing: Ask students to apply the concepts they have learned by locating advertisements in magazines or on television. Students will discuss their examples with the class. Consider if and how the technique encourages viewers to buy the product or service.

Assessment: Ask students to rewrite and redesign one advertisement using a different technique. Students should present their new ads and explain why they selected the alternative technique. Consider if and why the new advertisement is effective in persuading consumers to buy the product or service. A multiple-choice quiz can also assess student understanding of the terms and definitions.

ACTIVITY

4.11   Cross Marketing and the Big Five

Standard 19:   Media-literate communicators demonstrate knowledge and understanding of the commercial nature of media.

Grade Levels: 11–12

Description: Students research one of five media conglomerates and trace the marketing of one popular children's product.

Objective: Students will gain awareness of the prevalence of media conglomerates and their effects on cross promotion.

Materials: Internet access, magazines, television, writing utensils

Procedure: The cross marketing of products is more common today than in past years. Current ownership patterns encourage cross promotion of products, services, and talent. This is most readily observed during the holiday season, when products are promoted using a variety of media channels simultaneously.

1. Explain to students that at one time more than 50 companies dominated the production and distribution of media products. Over the past few years, media organizations have merged, forming a small handful of communications conglomerates. The top five major media conglomerates own the following types of organizations: publishing, music, television, radio, film production and distribution, magazines, sports teams, and a variety of other media outlets.

2. Divide the class into small groups and ask the groups to research one of the following organizations: AOL/Time Warner, News Corp., Viacom, Vivendi Universal, Walt Disney.

3. Have the students use the Internet and the library to research the following questions:

   a. Does the organization own any magazines, book or newspaper publishing companies, Internet service providers, music labels, sports teams, or telecommunication firms? If so, what are they?

   b. What film distribution and/or production companies does the organization own?

   c. Does the organization own any music companies or television stations? If so, what are they? Name specific programs or music groups.

   d. Have you noticed any products marketed in more than one of these venues? For example, are movies produced by one of the subsidiary organizations advertised on a television station owned by the parent company?

   e. Does the organization own a consumer products division? What types of products do they sell (toys, clothing, computer software, etc.)?

   f. How much money did the organization and/or its subsidiaries generate last year?

Debriefing: Have students present their findings to the class. Discuss the implications of a few organizations owning and producing most of the media we see, hear, and read. What are the positive and negative impacts of concentrated ownership? List these on the board. Discuss how ownership patterns may affect the free flow of information.

Assessment: As media industries merge to form fewer and fewer organizations, the opportunity to cross market products and talent increases. Have students locate a popular children's product produced by one of the five conglomerates and identify the media outlets used to market it (magazines, television programs, Internet, etc.). Students should present examples of what they've found and be able to discuss the social and economic implications of concentrated ownership in the marketing of children's products.

ACTIVITY

4.12   The Medium and the Message

Standard 20:   Media-literate communicators demonstrate the ability to use media to communicate to specific audiences.

Grade Levels: 7–8, 9–10

Description: This activity provides students with an awareness of the symbol systems used in different media and the opportunity to develop a prosocial message for peers in their community.

Objective: Students will identify symbol systems used to design persuasive narratives in different media and will use them to create a prosocial public service message for peers.

Materials: Writing materials, "The Medium and the Message" worksheet

Procedure: Different media employ different codes and symbol systems to move a story along or to get a message across.

1. Ask students to plan a short public service message for their peers, using one or more narrative techniques. This assignment could be planned for any of the following formats: a comic strip, illustrated story, radio announcement, television announcement, computer-generated message with computer graphics, animation, interactive video game, or interactive Web site.

2. Select topics from real issues that impact students (such as teasing, tolerance of individual differences, school violence and other school issues, environmental issues, and smoking). Have the students select one issue for the entire class and work in teams to plan their message for a specific medium.

3. Working in teams, students should think about the techniques and message that would appeal to and be effective in influencing an audience of their peers. Depending on the medium of choice, students may require help learning about the codes and conventions. You can provide examples of content from a variety of media to highlight these codes and conventions. In addition, you or a library media specialist can work with students to conduct research to answer some of the following questions for the given medium:

   a. What are some ways of setting the mood?

   b. How can you indicate whose point of view is being shown?

   c. How do you show movement?

   d. How do you draw the audience's attention to something?

   e. How can you use your equipment (camera angles, camera movement, type of shot, sound effects, color, music, interactive features) to convey information and feelings?

   f. What about words and writing? How can you use language effectively in different media to tell the story within the constraints and limits of your medium?

   g. How can you use silence to convey a message?

   h. How do you convey a passage of time?

      i. How do you indicate that something is being communicated as a memory?

      j. How do you convey the future?

Debriefing: Have students share their plans with the class, putting particular emphasis on difficulties, decision making, problem solving, and compromises they encountered in the planning process and how they took their audience into account. If the class decides to proceed to the production stage for a project, the appropriate tools will be needed, along with help from a teacher or library media specialist in how to use equipment safely and effectively.

Assessment: Have students react to one another's plans. Ask them to write about the limits of a given medium for relating a message. They should understand that there is more than one way to present a particular message. Use the "Medium and the Message" worksheet for students to evaluate their classmates' plans. Teachers should feel free to modify the worksheet.

The Medium and the Message

Rate production plans on a 1 to 5 scale for the following qualities as relevant to plans:

Poor		**Fair**		**Excellent**
1	2	3	4	5

_____ 1. Content of the message

_____ 2. Overall plans for using the medium

_____ 3. Use of text, dialogue, narration

_____ 4. Use of music

_____ 5. Use of animation

_____ 6. Use of camera movement

_____ 7. Use of sound effects

_____ 8. Attention to setting the mood

_____ 9. Use of silence

_____ 10. Overall effectiveness of the message

ACTIVITY

4.13 In the News

Standard 20: Media-literate communicators demonstrate the ability to use media to communicate to specific audiences.

Grade Levels: 9–10, 11–12

Description: This activity gives students the opportunity to investigate and write a news story for a specific audience using the basic questions of news writing.

Objective: Students will define what news is, recognize the differences between hard and soft news, identify the basic questions of news writing, and write a news story for broadcast or print.

Materials: Local and national newspapers, radio news broadcast, writing utensils

Procedure:
1. Discuss with students the definition of the term "news." Introduce students to the basic questions of news writing: Who? What? Where? When? Why and how? Identify the difference between hard and soft news.
   a. Hard news: usually found on the front page and is fact based
      - Timeliness—When did the event occur? News should be new. Old news is not news.
      - Significance of the Event or Consequence—How or why is the event important to the audience?
      - Closeness or Proximity—Where did the event happen? How close is it to home?
   b. Soft news: mostly consists of human-interest stories and features about people, trends, and other entertainment-related topics
      - Importance of the People Involved—Who is the story about? Is the person famous or well-known? Did he or she do something important or interesting?
      - Drama or "Human Interest"—Why is the event dramatic, entertaining, or interesting?
2. Using a newspaper, ask students to locate examples of each news type. Have them identify the language, vocabulary, and content of the story that classifies it as either hard or soft news, including subclassification information (timeliness, significance, proximity, people, or human interest).

Debriefing: Invite students to discuss how events and people become newsworthy. Discuss with students why this can be problematic at times. Call attention to the fact that people are responsible for selecting stories and that not all stories are equally selected. Explore how issues, ideas, and individuals can be constructed from different points of view. Encourage students to discuss how the purpose of a communication and its intended audience influence how it is constructed.

Discuss similarities and differences between broadcast and print news. Have students share the stories they have identified from each category, and discuss differences and similarities among them. For example, how does the locality of the paper influence the stories selected as news?

Discuss the headlines or teasers and how they are used to gain attention. Using actual news stories, ask students to rewrite the headlines. How does the wording of the headline or teaser change the appeal of the story?

Assessment: Each student should write two news stories, one for radio broadcast and the other for print or newspaper distribution, using the basic questions of news writing. An alternative is to have students write two different types of a news story (national interest story and close to home). Students should select the story/event/person and explain why it was identified as newsworthy. Have students present both stories and explain how the channel of distribution (broadcast or print) altered what information was included. Assessment should be based on the selection of topic, use of the six questions, the headline or teaser, and the appropriateness of story based on its channel of distribution or type.

ACTIVITY

4.14 I'm Your Candidate!

Standard 20: Media-literate communicators demonstrate the ability to use media to communicate to specific audiences.

Grade Levels: 11–12

Description: In this activity, students learn how media can be used to persuade and inform specific audiences by designing and implementing an election campaign for a fictitious or real candidate.

Objective: Students will demonstrate the ability to persuade and inform audiences, by selecting and organizing information tailored to the interests of specific demographic groups.

Materials: Examples of political communication, such as newspaper and magazine articles, campaign brochures, press releases, billboards, buttons, and so forth.

Procedure: Every four years, millions of U.S. citizens vote for president of the United States. Candidates use television, newspapers, radio, billboards, and Web sites to persuade voters.

1. Explain to students they are responsible for the design and implementation of an election campaign for a fictitious or real candidate.

2. Provide students with information about the candidate. A student election can be substituted for the fictitious candidate. For example, you may state the following types of information:

   Candidate's Name—Donald T. Drake

   Educational Achievements—B.S., State University (Business); J.D., Seton University

   Born—October 28, 1944

   Family Info.—married for 32 years to college sweetheart, Daisy. Three male children, ages 24, 28, and 30

   Professional Affiliations—former treasurer of the National Rifle Association; Boy Scout Leader

   Offices Held—governor, 4 years; State Senate, 15 years; mayor, 5 years

   Position on Taxes—believes in lower taxes for the wealthy

   Negative Info—not very active in high school; often disruptive; suspended for unknown reasons

   Position on Education—believes in statewide and national testing yearly

   Additional Information—wants to lower the cost of prescription drugs and raise the minimum wage; has worked to help senior citizens receive social security

   Assign students to work on one of three different demographic voting group committees. For example, students can work in groups that target voters in the following demographic groups: men and women ages 18 to 25, men and women over 65, and professional Hispanic women ages 30 to 40 living in New York City.

   If a student election is used, students can identify various interest groups within the student population (athletes, musicians, working students, etc.).

2. In teams or committees, have students design and develop catchy slogans, brochures, flyers, print and broadcast advertisements, billboards, and/or Web sites (as resources and time permit).

Debriefing: Students should develop a print advertisement, billboard, television advertisement, and Web site or radio advertisement targeting their specific population. The choice of medium should relate to the demographic. Discuss how the candidate's message changes depending on the demographic of the voters and the medium. Why does the target audience matter when developing communications? Have students present their communication and consider how well each group's message reached the target audience and its goal.

Assessment: Was the campaign effective? Were communication channels appropriate for the intended audience? Did the content reflect the interests of the voters? Communications should be evaluated on their complexity, diversity, and appropriateness.

TEACHING RESOURCES

TOOLS, TIPS, AND GREAT IDEAS

The following resources are organized according to professional organizations and resources for each major competency area (fundamentals, speaking, listening, and media literacy). Additional activities and assessment forms are included under each major competency area.

Professional Organizations

Teachers of communication can benefit greatly from membership in professional organizations. They can also make extremely important contributions to the discipline by their involvement in such organizations. The two organizations listed below are key in terms of providing resources for teaching and for curriculum development.

National Communication Association
1765 N Street N.W.
Washington, DC 20036
202-464-4622
FAX 202-464-4600
www.natcom.org

International Listening Association
Jim Pratt, Executive Director
Speech Communication and Theatre Department
University of Wisconsin–River Falls
410 S. 3rd Street
River Falls, WI 54022-5013
800-ILA-4505
www.listen.org

In addition to these national organizations, there are regional and state organizations. Regional organizations include the Central States Communication Association, the Eastern Communication Association, the Southern Speech Communication Association, and the Western Speech Communication Association. These all have Web sites and can be accessed through links on the National Communication Association Web site.

Fundamentals

PRINT RESOURCES

Allen, R., Brown, K., and Yatzin, J. (1985). *Learning Language through Communication: A Functional Approach.* Belmont, CA: Wadsworth.

Anderson, R., and Ross, V. (1998). *Questions of Communication.* New York: St. Martin's.

Backlund, P. (1985). "Essential Speaking and Listening Skills for Elementary School Students." *Communication Education* 34, pp. 185–195.

Barnes, D. (1992). *From Communication to Curriculum* (2nd ed.). Portsmouth, NH: Heinemann, Boynton/Cook.

Barnes, D., and Todd, F. (1995). *Communication and Learning Revisited.* Portsmouth, NH: Heinemann, Boynton/Cook.

Berko, R., Morreale, S., Cooper, P., and Perry, C. (1998). "Communication Standards and Competencies for Kindergarten through Grade 12: The Role of the National Communication Association." *Communication Education* 47 (2), pp. 174–182.

Calloway-Thomas, C., Cooper, P., and Blake, C. (1999). *Intercultural Communication: Roots and Routes.* Boston: Allyn and Bacon.

Chaney, A., and Burk, T. (1998). *Teaching Oral Communication in Grades K–8.* Boston: Allyn and Bacon.

Christ, W., ed. (1994). *Assessing Communication Education: A Handbook for Media, Speech and Theatre Educators.* Annandale, VA: National Communication Association.

Collins, R., and Cooper, P. (1997). *The Power of Story: Teaching through Storytelling* (2nd ed.). Boston: Allyn and Bacon.

Communication Teacher. This journal is published by and available from the National Communication Association.

Cooper, P., ed. (1992). *Activities for Teaching Speaking and Listening: Grades 7–12.* Annandale, VA: National Communication Association.

Cooper, P., ed. *Communication Competencies for Teachers.* Annandale, VA: National Communication Association.

Cooper, P., and Collins, R. (1991). "Using Storytelling to Teach Oral Communication Competencies K–12." *Illinois English Bulletin* 79, pp. 76–90.

Cooper, P., and Simonds, C. (2002). *Communication for the Classroom Teacher* (7th ed.). Boston: Allyn and Bacon.

Dance, F. (1970). "The 'Concept' of Communication." *Journal of Communication* 20 (2), pp. 201–210.

Daniel, A., ed. (1992). *Activities Integrating Oral Communication Skills for Students Grades K–8.* Annandale, VA: National Communication Association.

Dickson, W., ed. (1981). *Children's Oral Communication Skills.* New York: Academic.

Elliott, N., ed. (1984). "Special Issue: Children's Communication Development." *Western Journal of Speech Communication* 48, pp. 105–196.

Galvin, K., and Book, C. (1998). *Person to Person.* Lincolnwood, IL: NTC/Contemporary.

Galvin, K., and Cooper, P. (1999). *The Basics of Speech* (3rd ed.). Lincolnwood, IL: NTC/Contemporary.

Griffin, E. (2000). *A First Look at Communication Theory.* New York: McGraw-Hill.

Hall, B., Morreale, S., and Gaudino, J. (1999). "A Survey of the Status of Oral Communication in the K–12 Public Education System." *Communication Education* 48 (2), pp. 139–148.

Hay, E. (1992). *Program Assessment in Oral Communication.* Annandale, VA: National Communication Association.

Hay, E., ed. (1992). *Speech Resources: Exercises and Activities* (2nd ed.). Los Angeles: Roxbury.

Hay, L., and Zboray, R. (1992). *Complete Communication Skills Activities Kit.* West Nyack, NY: Center for Applied Research in Education.

Hunsaker, R. (1990). *Oral Communication: Speaking and Listening* (2nd ed.). Englewood, CO: Morton.

Kepler, P., Royse, B., and Kepler, J. (1996). *Windows to the World.* Glenview, IL: Good Year Books.

Knapp, M., and Hall, J. (1997). *Nonverbal Communication in Human Interaction* (4th ed.). Philadelphia: Harcourt, Brace, Jovanovich.

Larson, C., Backlund, P., Redmond, M., and Barbour, A. (1978). *Assessing Functional Communication.* Annandale, VA: National Communication Association.

Modaff, J., and Hopper, R. (1984). "Why Speech is 'Basic.'" *Communication Education* 33, pp. 37–42.

Morreale, S., and Backlund, P. (1996). *Large Scale Assessment of Oral Communication: K–12 and Higher Education* (2nd ed.). Annandale, VA: National Communication Association.

Morreale, S., Osborn, M., and Pearson, J. (2000). "Why Communication Is Important: A Rationale for the Centrality of the Study of Communication." *Journal of the Association for Communication Administration* 29, pp. 1–25.

Most, M. (1994). "Certification Standards for Speech Communication Teachers: A Nationwide Survey." *Communication Education* 43, pp. 195–204.

Myers, V., and Herndon, R. (1988). *Dynamics of Speech: Toward Effective Communication.* Lincolnwood, IL: National Textbook.

National Communication Association. "The Competent Speaker Speech Evaluation Form." Annandale, VA: National Communication Association.

National Communication Association. (2000). *K–12 Curriculum Guidelines.* Annandale, VA: National Communication Association.

National Communication Association. (1992). *K–12 Oral Communication Teacher Training Workshop Manual* (Volumes 1–5). Annandale, VA: National Communication Association.

O'Connor, J. (1996). *Exploring Communication* (4th ed.). Lincolnwood, IL: National Textbook.

Popp, M. (1996). *Teaching Language and Literature in Elementary Classrooms.* Mahwah, NJ: Erlbaum.

Samovar, L., and Porter, R. (2000). *Communication Between Cultures* (9th ed.). Belmont, CA: Wadsworth.

Seiler, W., and Beall, M. (1999). *Communication: Making Connections.* Boston: Allyn and Bacon.

Stewart, J., and Logan, C. (1993). *Together: Communicating Interpersonally* (4th ed.). New York: McGraw-Hill.

Wiemann, M., and Wiemann, J. (1975). *Nonverbal Communication in the Elementary Classroom.* Urbana, IL: ERIC Clearinghouse on Reading and Communication Skills.

Wilbrand, M., and Rieke, R. (1983). *Teaching Oral Communication in Elementary Schools.* New York: Macmillan.

Wood, B. (1977). *Development of Functional Communication Competencies: Grades 7–12.* Urbana, IL: ERIC Clearinghouse on Reading and Communication Skills.

Wood, B. (1977). *Development of Functional Communication Competencies: Pre-K–Grade 6.* Urbana, IL: ERIC Clearinghouse on Reading and Communication Skills.

Speaking

PRINT RESOURCES

Barker, L., Wahlers, K., and Watson, K. (1995). *Groups in Process: An Introduction to Small Group Communication* (5th ed.). Boston: Allyn and Bacon.

Cavanaugh, D. (1997). *Preparing Visual Aids for Presentations.* Boston: Allyn and Bacon.

Gronbeck, B., McKerrow, R., Ehninger, D., and Monroe, A. (1990). *Principles and Types of Speech Communication* (11th ed.). Glenview, IL: Scott Foresman/Little Brown Higher Education.

McCroskey, J., and Richmond, V. (1991). *Quiet Children and the Classroom Teacher.* Urbana, IL: ERIC Clearinghouse on Reading and Communication Skills.

McCroskey, J., Andersen, J., Richmond, V., and Wheeless, L. (1981). "Communication Apprehension of Elementary and Secondary Students and Teachers." *Communication Education* 30, pp. 122–132.

Payne, J., and Prentice, D. (1987). *Getting Started in Public Speaking.* Lincolnwood, IL: National Textbook.

Zarefsky, D. (1999). *Public Speaking: Strategies for Success* (2nd ed.). Boston: Allyn and Brown.

Ziefert, H. (1989). *When the TV broke.* New York: Puffin.

NONPRINT RESOURCES

Contact the following film producers and distributors for a list of nonprint resources for fundamentals and speaking.

AIMS Media
9710 De Soto Avenue
Chatsworth, CA 91311-4409
800-367-2467

Alfred Higgins Productions, Inc.
6350 Laurel Canyon Boulevard
North Hollywood, CA 91606
800-766-5353

Barr Films
12801 Schabarum Avenue
P.O. Box 7878
Irwindale, CA 91706-7878
800-234-7878

BFA Educational Media
2349 Chafee Drive
St. Louis, MO 63146
800-221-1274

Brigham Young University Media Service
101 Fletcher Building
Provo, UT 84602
800-378-4071

Carousel Films, Inc.
260 5th Avenue, Suite 405
New York, NY 10001
800-683-1660

CRM/McGraw-Hill Films
2215 Faraday Avenue
Carlsbad, CA 92008-7295
800-421-0833

Encyclopedia Britannica Educational Corporation
310 South Michigan Avenue
Chicago, IL 60604
800-554-9862

Great Plains National Television Library
University of Nebraska
Box 80669
Lincoln, NE 68501-0669
800-228-4630

Guidance Associates/The Center for Humanities, Inc.
Communications Parks, Box 1000
Mount Kisco, NY 10549
800-431-1242

Indiana University Instructional Support Services
Bloomington, IN 47405-5901
800-552-8620

International Medifilms
14155 Magnolia Boulevard, Suite 344
Sherman Oaks, CA 91423
818-386-1818

Iowa State University
Media Resources Center
121 Pearson Hall
Ames, IA 50011
800-447-0060

Pyramid
Box 1048
Santa Monica, CA 90406
800-421-2304

Salinger Films
1635 12th Street
Santa Monica, CA 90404
800-775-5025

This list was compiled by Andrew Wolvin and Carolyn Coakley.

Listening

PRINT RESOURCES

Bozik, M., and Carlin, D. (1989). *Listen! A Read-Aloud, Listening to Literature Program.* Sundance Educational Materials.

Galvin, K. (1985). *Listening By Doing.* Lincolnwood, IL: National Textbook.

Hunsaker, R. (1989). "What Listening Skills Should Be Taught to Teachers and Students?" *The Future of Speech Communication Education,* Galvin, K., and Cooper, P. (Eds.), (pp. 27–30). Annandale, VA: National Communication Association.

Phillips, A., Lipson, A., and Basseches, M. (1994). "Empathy and Listening Skills: A Development Perspective on Learning to Listen." *Interdisciplinary Handbook of Adult Lifespan Learning,* J. Sinnott (Ed.), (pp. 301–324). Westport, CT: Greenwood.

Wolvin, A., and Coakley, C. (1992). *Listening* (4th ed.). Dubuque, IA: Wm. C. Brown.

The following books are available through the International Listening Association. They are not the only books about listening but are among those recognized as dealing mainly with effective listening skills. In addition, many other books that include chapters and units on listening as a skill are available.

Barker, L.L. (2000). *Listen Up: How to Improve Relationships, Reduce Stress, and Be More Productive by Using the Power of Listening.* New York: St. Martin's.

Barker, L.L. (1991). *Listening Behavior.* Silverthorne, CO: SPECTRA.

Barker, L.L., Steil, L.K., and Watson, K.W. (1983). *Effective Listening: Key to Your Success.* New York: McGraw-Hill Higher Education.

Bechler, L., and Weaver, R.L. (1994). *Listen to Win.* Sandy, OR: Mastermedia.

Borisoff, D. (1997). *Listening in Everyday Life: A Personal and Professional Approach.* Wellesley, MA: University Press of America.

Brownell, J. (1995). *Listening: Attitudes, Principles and Skills.* Englewood Cliffs, NJ: Prentice Hall.

Brownell, J. (1986). *Building Active Listening Skills.* Englewood Cliffs, NJ: Prentice Hall.

Burley-Allen, M. (1995). *Listening: The Forgotten Skill (A Self-Teaching Guide)* (also an audiotape available). New York: John Wiley.

Coakley, C.G. (1996). *Teaching Effective Listening: A Practical Guide for the High School Classroom.* Coakley Communication Connection. River Falls, WI: International Listening Association.

Coakley, C.G. (1989). *Experiential Listening: Tools for Teachers and Trainers.* Silverthorne, CO: SPECTRA.

Garman, C.G., and Garman, J.F. (1992). *Teaching Young Children Effective Listening Skills.* York, PA: William Gladden Foundation.

Halley, R. (1999). *How Audiences Listen: Critical Information for the Public Speaker.* Columbia, MO: Kaia.

Halley, R. (1997). *And Then I Was Surprised by What You Said: The Impact of Love and Listening on Community.* Columbia, MO: Kaia.

Lundsteen, S.W. (1979). *Listening: Its Impact at All Levels on Reading and Other Language Arts.* National Council of Teachers of English.

Nichols, R.G. (1960). *Are You Listening?* (audiocassette). River Falls, WI: International Listening Association.

Steil, L.K. (1982). *Listening Training and Development: Guidelines for Human Resource Professionals.* River Falls, WI: International Listening Association.

Steil, L.K., Miller, R.F., and Wasley, J.K. (1982). *Effective Listening.* Hopkins, MN: Telstar.

Steil, L.K., et al. (1985). *Listening: It Can Change Your Life.* New York: McGraw-Hill.

Steil, L.K., et al. (1983). *Effective Listening: Key to Your Success.* New York: McGraw-Hill Higher Education.

Watson, K.W., and Barker, L.L. (1995). *Managing by Listening Around.* Silverthorne, CO: SPECTRA.

Watson, K.W., and Barker, L.L. (1995). *Listen Up: Learning Activities.* San Francisco, CA: Jossey-Bass.

Wolff, F.I., Marsnik, N.C., Tracey, W.S., and Nichols, R.G. (1983). *Perceptive Listening.* Ft. Worth, TX: Harcourt College.

Wolvin, A.D., and Coakley, C.G. (1999). *Listening* (6th ed.). New York: McGraw Hill.

NONPRINT RESOURCES

Devereaux, R. (1999). *Power Listening for Problem Solvers* (audiocassette). River Falls, WI: International Listening Association.

Devereaux, R. (1998). *Power Listening for Parents* (audiocassette). River Falls, WI: International Listening Association.

Devereaux, R. (1997). *Power Listening* (audiocassette). River Falls, WI: International Listening Association.

Media Literacy

PRINT RESOURCES

Acuff, D.S. (1997). *What Kids Buy and Why: The Psychology of Marketing to Kids.* New York: Free Press.

Anderson, N. (1989). *Media Works.* Toronto: Oxford University Press.

Bilowit, D.W. (1981). *Critical Television Viewing: Language Skills Work-a-Text.*

Bruner, J. (1990). *Acts of Meaning.* Cambridge: Harvard University Press.

Brunner, C., and Tally, W. (1999). *The New Media Literacy Handbook: An Educator's Guide to Bringing Media Literacy into the Classroom.* New York: Random House.

Buckingham, D. (1996). *Moving Images: Understanding Children's Emotional Responses to Television.* New York: Manchester University Press.

Buckingham, D. (1990). *Watching Media Learning: Making Sense of Media Education.* London: Falmer.

Christ, W.G., and Potter, W.J. (1998). "Media Literacy, Media Education, and the Academy." *Journal of Communication* 48 (1).

Considine, D., and Haley, G.E. (1999). *Visual Messages: Integrating Imagery into Instruction: A Media Literacy Resource for Teachers.* Englewood, CO: Teacher Ideas Press.

Dell Vecchio, G. (1997). *Creating Ever-Cool: A Marketer's Guide to a Kid's Heart.* Pelican Publishing.

Ewen, S. (1988). *All Consuming Images: The Politics of Style in Contemporary Culture.* New York: Basic Books.

Healy, J.M. (1990). *Endangered Minds: Why Children Don't Think and What We Can Do About It.* New York: Touchstone.

Heart, A., ed. (1998). *Teaching the Media: International Perspectives.* New York: Lawrence Erlbaum.

Hirschman, E. (2000). *Heroes, Monsters, and Meddiahs: Movies and Television Shows as the Mythology of American Culture.* Andrews McMeel.

Hobbs, R. (1998). "The Seven Great Debates in the Media Literacy Movement." *Journal of Communication* 48 (1).

Kilbourne, J. (1999). *Deadly Persuasion: Why Women and Girls Must Fight the Addictive Power of Advertising.* New York: Free Press.

Kruger, E., and Christel, M.T. (2001). *Seeing and Believing: How to Teach Media Literacy in the English Classroom.* New York: Heinemann.

Kubey, R., ed. (1997). *Media Literacy in the Information Age.* New Brunswick, NJ: Transaction.

Kubey, R., and Csikszentmihalyi, M. (1990). *Television and the Quality of Life: How Viewing Shapes Everyday Experience.* Lawrence Erlbaum.

Lockwood-Summers, S. (2000). *Media Alert: 200 Activities to Create Media-Savvy Kids.* Littleton, CO: Media Alert!.

Masterman, L. (1985). *Teaching the Media.* London: Routledge.

Masterman, L., and Mariet, F. (1994). *Media Education in 1990's Europe: A Teacher's Guide.* The Netherlands: Council of Europe Press; Croton, NY: Manhattan Publishing.

McLuhan, M. (1964). *Understanding the Media: The Extension of Man.* New York: McGraw-Hill.

McLuhan, M., Hutchon, M., and McLuhan, E. (1977). *City as Classroom: Understanding Language and Media.* Ontario: Book Society.

Pungente, J., and O'Malley, M.O. (1999). *More than Meets the Eye: Watching Television Watching Us.* Ontario: McClelland & Stewart.

Silverblatt, A. (1995). *Media Literacy: Keys to Interpreting Media Messages.* Praeger.

Singer, D.G., and Singer, J.L., eds. (2001). *Handbook of Children and the Media.* Thousand Oaks, CA: Sage.

Singer, D.G., Singer, J.E., and Zuckerman, D.M. (1981). *Getting the Most Out of TV.* Santa Monica, CA: Good Year.

Strausburger, V. (1995). *Adolescents and the Media: Medical and Psychological Impact.* Thousand Oaks, CA: Sage.

Tyner, K. (1998). *Literacy in a Digital World: Teaching and Learning in the Age of Information.* Lawrence Erlbaum.

Worsnop, C. (1999). *Screening Images: Ideas for Media Education.* Ontario: Wright Communications.

ADVOCACY GROUPS AND WEB SITES

Alliance for a Media Literate America

www.nmec.org

The Alliance for a Media Literate America (AMLA) is committed to promoting media literacy education that is focused on critical inquiry, learning, and skill building rather than on media bashing and blame. This national, grassroots membership organization is a key force in bringing media literacy education to the 60 million students in the United States, their parents, their teachers, and others who care about youth.

Assignment: Media Literacy

www.assignmentmedialit.com

A comprehensive new curriculum resource designed to strengthen media literacy and communication skills and promote reading, writing, and critical thinking skills for students in grades K–12. Call 888-734-2328 to ask questions or get more information about the curriculum. Developed by Renee Hobbs, director of the Media Literacy Project and a professor of communication at Babson College in Wellesley, Massachusetts.

Center for Media Education

www.cme.org

The Center for Media Education is a national nonprofit organization dedicated to creating a quality electronic media culture for children and youth, their families, and the community. Contact: CME 2120 L Street, NW, Suite 200, Washington, DC 20037, 202-331-7833.

Center for Media Literacy

www.medialit.org

The Center for Media Literacy is dedicated to a new vision of literacy for the 21st century: the ability to communicate competently in all media forms, print and electronic, as well as to access, understand, analyze, and evaluate the powerful images, words, and sounds that make up our contemporary mass media culture. Contact: Center for Media Literacy, 4727 Wilshire Blvd., #403, Los Angeles, CA 90010, 800-226-9494.

Center for Media Studies

www.mediastudies.rutgers.edu

The Center for Media Studies at Rutgers University, New Brunswick, New Jersey, is concerned with the impact of media on contemporary society. Through research, teaching, public events, and outreach, the center seeks ways for the media to better serve the public interest. Contact: Robert Kubey, Ph.D., director, media@scils.rutgers.edu, Center for Media Studies, SCILS, Rutgers University, 4 Huntington Street, New Brunswick, NJ 08901-1071.

Children Now: Children and the Media Program

www.childrennow.org

This is a nonprofit, nonpartisan group that speaks on behalf of children and their families. The organization aims to improve the quality of news and entertainment media for children.

Just Think Foundation

www.justthink.org

The Just Think Foundation (JTF) is a dynamic nonprofit, dedicated to teaching young people literacy for the 21st century by providing them with the skills to be critical thinkers and creative producers.

Media Awareness Network

www.media-awareness.ca

The Media Awareness Network offers practical support for media education in the home, school, and community and provides information and "food for thought" on our fast-evolving media culture. It is also a place where educators, parents, students, and community workers can share resources and explore ways to make media a more positive force in children's lives.

Media Literacy Clearinghouse

www.med.sc.edu/medialit

This project is funded by the Joint Legislative EIA Select Committee, as sponsor of the South Carolina Middle Grades Schools State Policy Initiative (SCMGSSPI) and is operated by the Office of Alcohol and Drug Studies, Department of Neuropsychiatry and Behavioral Science, School of Medicine, University of South Carolina, for the purpose of facilitating study of media literacy skills and health-related risks among young adolescents. The site is maintained by Frank Baker, media educator, Columbia, South Carolina, 800-277-3245, fbaker@scetv.org.

Media Literacy Online Project

http://interact.uoregon.edu/MediaLit/HomePage

This site provides many important readings and resources for teachers, parents, and caregivers. Contact: Gary Ferrington, director, Media Literacy Online Project, College of Education, University of Oregon, Eugene.

National Institute on Media and the Family

www.mediafamily.org

The National Institute on Media and the Family, founded by David Walsh, Ph.D., is a national resource for teachers, parents, community leaders, and other caring adults who are interested in the influence of electronic media on early childhood education, child development, academic performance, culture, and violence. Contact: Media and the Family, 606 24th Avenue S, Suite 606, Minneapolis, MN 55454, 888-672-5437.

National PTA: Family and Community Critical Viewing Project

www.pta.org

The Family and Community Critical Viewing Project, a partnership of the National PTA, the National Cable Television Association, and Cable in the Classroom, supports parents and teachers in promoting critical viewing.

National Telemedia Council

www.danenet.wicip.org/ntc

A professional, nonprofit organization promoting media literacy education through partnerships with educators, informed citizens, and media producers across the country. Contact: Marieli Rowe, 120 E. Wilson Street, Madison, WI 53703, ntc@danenet.wicip.org.

Parents Television Council (PTC)

www.parentstv.org

The Parents Television Council (PTC) is a nonprofit organization dedicated solely to improving the quality of entertainment programming, with emphasis on television. Contact: Parents Television Council, 707 Wilshire Boulevard #1950, Los Angeles, CA 90017, 213-629-9255.

Project Look Sharp

www.ithaca.edu/looksharp

Project Look Sharp is an initiative to promote and support the integration of media literacy into classroom curricula at all grade levels and instructional areas, as well as to evaluate the effectiveness of media literacy education in schools. Contact: Project Look Sharp, 1119 Williams Hall, Ithaca College, Ithaca, NY 14850-7390.

CHILDREN'S LITERATURE

Angell, J. (1979). *A Word from Our Sponsor, or My Friend Alfred.* Scarsdale, NY: Bradbury Press.

Brown, M. (1995). *Arthur's TV Trouble.* Toronto: Little, Brown.

Brown, M., and Brown, L.K. (1984). *The Bionic Bunny Show.* Boston: Atlantic Monthly.

Berenstein, S., and Berenstein, J. (1984). *The Berenstein Bears and Too Much TV.* New York: Random House.

Gibbons, G. (1985). *Lights! Camera! Action!* New York: Harper & Row.

Miles, B. (1976). *The TV Kid.* Toronto: Penguin Books.

Jenkins, P. (1991). *Flipbook Animation.* Toronto: Kids Can.

Schartz, A. (1982). *Bea and Mr. Jones.* New York: Bradbury.

Waber, B. (1994). *Lyle at the Office.* Boston: Houghton Mifflin.

Winn, C.M. (1996). *Box-Head Boy.* Minneapolis: Fairview.

Additional Teaching Materials: Junior and Senior High School Level

FUNDAMENTALS

Communication Journal

Often, students need time for reflection about communication theory as it relates to their lives. They also need to analyze their own communication and that of others in order to improve their communication competence. Asking students to keep a journal in which they record their own ideas about communication can be very helpful. Below are some suggested journal assignments:

1. Think about a time in which your first impression of a person was wrong. What led you to that perception? What caused you to change your perception?

2. Collect quotes and/or cartoons that relate to communication.

3. People develop biases related to the culture in which they live. What are some of your biases? How will these affect your communication?

4. Read a fairytale or view a television sitcom. What gender stereotypes are communicated? How do these affect communication between the sexes?

5. What is your favorite family story? Why?

6. Watch a television sitcom without the sound. What information do you get from just the nonverbal communication? For example, what do posture and body position tell you about a person's status and attitude toward others?

7. Tape-record your voice. List qualities you like. List those you don't like. Write goals for the improvement of your voice.

Nonverbal Observation

Since nonverbal communication is an extremely important part of the communication process, students should be encouraged to become aware of it. Ask students to complete the Nonverbal Observation Form (see next page) several times throughout the term.

Nonverbal Observation Form

Situation observed (where, when, people involved, etc.): _____

_____

Cue	Observations	Interpretation
Appearance	_____	_____
Movement	_____	_____
Gestures	_____	_____
Facial Expression	_____	_____
Eye Contact	_____	_____
Spatial Relations	_____	_____
Touch	_____	_____
Artifacts	_____	_____
Voice (Pitch, tone, volume)	_____	_____
Other	_____	_____

Self-Collage

Make a collage of yourself. Organize it around the four components of self-concept: how you see yourself, how you would like to see yourself, how you think other people see you, and how you would like others to see you.

Self-Disclosure Impromptus

On 3 x 5 inch index cards, write one of the following topics on each card:

My favorite movie _____

My favorite pet _____

My favorite book _____

My favorite thing to do for fun _____

My most embarrassing moment _____

The person I admire most is _____ because _____

The vacation I liked best _____

Students draw a topic from a hat and deliver a short (one- to three-minute) speech about that topic.

Group Participant Evaluation Form

Whenever students work in groups you can evaluate their performance as a group member. The following is an example assessment form.

Group Participant Evaluation Form

Name: _____

Rate the participant using:

5 = superior   4 = excellent   3 = average   2 = below average   1 = poor

Criteria   **Rating**

1. Attitude: Open-minded, objective, willing to modify views when presented
   with new evidence   _____

2. Knowledge: Understood the issue under discussion, showed skill in sharing
   information   _____

3. Thinking: Analyzed the issue for discussion well, able to develop relationships
   between ideas   _____

4. Listening: Kept track of the discussion and comments made by others,
   avoided irrelevant or repetitive contributions   _____

5. Speaking: Expressed ideas clearly and concisely   _____

6. Spontaneity: Reacted to what was happening at the time, did not merely
   recite preprepared remarks   _____

7. Consideration: Was courteous of others, disagreed without being disagreeable,
   avoided dominating the discussion, interested in helping the group reach its goal   _____

Additional Comments:

_____

_____

_____

Grade: _____

Intercultural Stories

These activities help students understand other cultures through storytelling.

1. Each student tells a myth, legend, or folktale from a specific culture. The discussion that follows centers on (1) the student's performance (using one of the evaluation forms below), (2) the cultural value communicated by the story.

2. Each student writes and tells a fable. Discussion focuses on the cultural value communicated in the fable and the effect this value has on communication with others.

3. Have students read the book *Mai Pen Rai Means Never Mind,* by Carol Hollinger (1993). This is the story of an American woman's experience living in Thailand. Next have students read a children's book by Emily Cheney Neville, *The China Year* (1991), the story of a young American girl's experience living in China. For comparison have students read *In the Year of the Boar and Jackie Robinson* (Lord, 1984), the story of a young Chinese girl who moves to America. Using the experiences they read about in the books, students create their own stories. For example, students could take a character in one of the books and tell a story about her 10 years after the book's story ends.

Storytelling Evaluation Form 1

Storyteller's Name _____

Story's Title _____

1. Introduction: Was mood set? Was place set? Was time set? Were characters clear?

_____

_____

2. Story: Was it appropriate for the audience? Did it seem believable? Was the story concise, tight, and held together? Was it fresh, new, entertaining? Was the story told well in terms of use of language, use of body and gestures, use of voice?

_____

_____

3. Additional Comments:

_____

_____

_____

Grade: _____

Storytelling Evaluation Form 2

If possible, videotape each storyteller telling a story. Classmates and the teller can then critique and compare critiques using this form.

The storyteller was (1) able to, (2) sometimes able to, (3) not able to:

Motivate the audience to listen   _____

Convey action vividly   _____

Convey sequences of events clearly   _____

Assume character's point of view   _____

Express human motives   _____

Express human conflict   _____

Express human values   _____

Establish mood   _____

Use figurative language   _____

Use language rhythmically   _____

Speak clearly and distinctly   _____

Utilize varied intonation   _____

Utilize appropriate gestures   _____

Utilize eye contact effectively   _____

End the story gracefully   _____

Grade: _____

SPEAKING

Speech Evaluation Forms

The following forms can be used to evaluate student speeches.

Speaker's Self-Evaluation Form

Name _____   Speech _____

Upon completion of the speech, take a few moments to reflect on and think about your research, organization, and delivery. If you were to give this speech again, what would you do differently? Why? What would you retain? How would you evaluate yourself? Be specific in your comments—do not say things such as "It was fine" or "I would keep it as it was." These are not helpful statements.

Topic Selection:

_____

_____

Research:

_____

_____

Appropriateness to you, the classroom, and the specific audience:

_____

_____

Organization—introduction, body, conclusion; transitions; internal summaries:

_____

_____

Explanation and clarity of ideas:

_____

_____

(continued)

Speaker's Self-Evaluation *continued*

Supporting materials:

_____

_____

Use of language:

_____

_____

Visual delivery—movement, eye contact, gestures:

_____

_____

Vocal delivery—conversational style, sincerity, variety, ease of listening:

_____

_____

How did you adapt the speech to this audience?

_____

_____

_____

What would you change? Why?

_____

_____

_____

What would you retain? Why?

_____

_____

_____

Informative Speech Evaluation

Name _____   Date _____

Topic _____   Time _____

The following criteria will be used to evaluate your speech. 1 is very low or poor; 2 is fair; 3 is average; 4 is good; 5 is excellent.

Topic Choice   5 4 3 2 1

 Appropriate for the speaker? Audience? Assignment?

Content   5 4 3 2 1

 Ideas well developed? Support provided? Adequate number
 of sources? Oral footnotes? Content makes sense?

Organization   5 4 3 2 1

 Clear, effective introduction? Transitions provided? Easy to
 follow? Conclusion summarizes and synthesizes?

Language Use   5 4 3 2 1

 Appropriate for speaker? Situation? Classroom? Grammatically
 correct? Correct pronunciation?

Physical Delivery   5 4 3 2 1

 Good eye contact? Appropriate posture/gestures/movement?
 Appropriate facial expression?

Vocal Delivery   5 4 3 2 1

 Appropriate volume? Effective vocal variety? Appropriate rate? Pauses
 used appropriately? Pitch/Quality appropriate for speaker/situation?

Total Points received _____

Total Points possible   30

Comments/suggestions for future speeches:

_____

_____

_____

Persuasive Speech Evaluation

Name _____   Date _____

Topic _____   Time _____

The following criteria will be used to evaluate your speech. 1 is low, and the higher the number, the better you have met the criterion.

Topic Selection   5 4 3 2 1

Appropriate for audience, classroom, assignment, speaker?

Research   5 4 3 2 1

Appropriate amount? Appropriate types? Provides an evaluation of
Web sources? Adequate number of sources cited in body of speech
to demonstrate the significance of the research completed?

Organization   5 4 3 2 1

Introduction stimulated interest and provided clear direction? Body
organized and easy to follow? Conclusion clearly signaled an end to the
speech, provided a summary, provided listeners with a memorable thought?

Explanation and Clarity of Ideas   5 4 3 2 1

Supporting material adequate? Fully and clearly developed? Persuasive?
Language clear and appropriate?

Delivery   5 4 3 2 1

Adequate and appropriate movement, eye contact, gestures, facial
expressions? Conversational style? Sincere? Adequate volume? Vocal variety?

Comments/suggestions for future speeches:

_____

_____

_____

_____

Total Points received _____

Demonstration Speech Evaluation

Name _____   Date _____

Topic _____   Time _____

Each category is rated on a 1–5 scale, with 5 as the highest rating.

Analysis

Speech narrow enough to be fully developed in time allotted? Appropriate for demonstration method? Appropriate for audience?

Rating _____

Supporting materials

Visual aids were appropriate? Used correctly? Utilized sufficient clarifying materials (examples, illustrations, etc.)?

Rating _____

Organization

Introduction gained audience attention, created interest, oriented audience to speech, included a clear and precise thesis statement? Body of the speech was clearly organized and easy to follow, transitions provided necessary links between ideas, utilized appropriate signposts and internal summaries? Conclusion summarized the speech content, provided a link back to introductory comments, and provided an idea for the audience to remember?

Rating _____

Total Rating _____

Communication Apprehension

Competent speakers demonstrate the ability to manage communication apprehension. The PRCA-24 instrument included here can be administered to your students so that they can determine their level of communication apprehension. The activity that follows on p. 134 should be provided for student reflection on the topic of anxiety.

PERSONAL REPORT OF COMMUNICATION APPREHENSION (PRCA-24)

Because we know that many teachers, as well as students, have high levels of communication apprehension, it is important for you to determine your own level of communication apprehension. In order to do this, complete the following Personal Report of Communication Apprehension (McCroskey & Richmond, 1991, pp. 31–33).

Directions: This instrument is composed of 24 statements concerning feelings about communicating with other people. Please indicate the degree to which each statement applies to you by marking whether you (1) Strongly Agree, (2) Agree, (3) Are Undecided, (4) Disagree, or (5) Strongly Disagree. There are no right or wrong answers. Answer quickly; record your first impression.

_____   1. I dislike participating in group discussions.

_____   2. Generally, I am comfortable while participating in group discussions.

_____   3. I am tense and nervous while participating in group discussions.

_____   4. I like to get involved in group discussions.

_____   5. Engaging in a group discussion with new people makes me tense and nervous.

_____   6. I am calm and relaxed when I am called upon to express an opinion at a meeting.

_____   7. Generally, I am nervous when I have to participate in a meeting.

_____   8. Usually, I am calm and relaxed while participating in meetings.

_____   9. I am calm and relaxed when I am called upon to express an opinion at a meeting.

_____   10. I am afraid to express myself at meetings.

_____   11. Communicating at meetings usually makes me feel uncomfortable.

_____   12. I am relaxed when answering questions at a meeting.

_____   13. While participating in a conversation with a new acquaintance, I feel very nervous.

_____   14. I have no fear of speaking up in conversations.

_____   15. Ordinarily, I am very tense and nervous in conversations.

_____   16. Ordinarily, I am very calm and relaxed in conversations.

_____   17. While conversing with a new acquaintance, I feel very relaxed.

_____   18. I'm afraid to speak up in conversations.

_____   19. I have no fear of giving a speech.

_____   20. Certain parts of my body feel tense and rigid while giving a speech.   *(continued)*

PRCA-24 continued

_____ 21. I feel relaxed while giving a speech.

_____ 22. My thoughts become confused and jumbled when I am giving a speech.

_____ 23. I face the prospect of giving a speech with confidence.

_____ 24. While giving a speech, I get so nervous I forget facts I really know.

The PRCA-24 permits computation of one total score and four subscores. The subscores are related to communication apprehension in each of four common communication contexts: group discussions, meetings, interpersonal conversations, and public speaking. To compute your scores, add or subtract your scores for each item as indicated below.

1. Group Discussions
    18 (plus) scores for items 2, 4, and 6;
    (minus) scores for items 1, 3, and 5.   Subtotal _____

2. Meetings
    18 (plus) scores for items 8, 9, and 12;
    (minus) scores for items 7, 10, and 11.   Subtotal _____

3. Interpersonal Conversations
    18 (plus) scores for items 14, 16, and 17;
    (minus) scores for items 13, 15, and 18.   Subtotal _____

4. Public Speaking
    18 (plus) scores for items 19, 21, and 23;
    (minus) scores for items 20, 22, and 24.   Subtotal _____

                                                   Total   _____

Scores on the four contexts (Group Discussions, Meetings, Interpersonal Conversations, and Public Speaking) can range from a low of 6 to a high of 30. Any score above 18 indicates some degree of apprehension. If your score is above 18 for the Public Speaking Context, you are like the overwhelming majority of Americans.

To obtain your total score for the PRCA-24, add your four subscores together. Your score should range between 24 and 120. If your score is below 24 or above 120, you have made a mistake in computing the score.

From J. McCroskey and V. Richmond, _Quiet Children and the Classroom Teacher_ (Bloomington, IN: ERIC, 1991) 27–30. Used by permission of the National Communication Association.

Managing Anxiety

Think about how you have managed or might manage your anxiety in a given communication situation. Identify three different ideas or strategies for managing your anxiety:

1. _____

2. _____

3. _____

Identify three different strategies that either your instructor or your classmates have suggested to help you manage anxiety:

1. _____

2. _____

3. _____

Interview another person (in person or by e-mail) who communicates frequently (teacher, principal, minister, priest, or rabbi, health care professional, radio or television personality, or a businessperson) and learn five strategies she/he uses to manage or overcome anxiety.

1. _____

2. _____

3. _____

4. _____

5. _____

Reflecting on Language and Speaking

Competent speakers remember who their listeners are and can place themselves in their listeners' perspectives. Competent speakers need to know how language affects the communication process and how language may affect their listeners. To help you understand how language affects listeners, complete the following:

Identify three language choices you have made in the past because you were aware of your listeners and their perspectives.

1. _____

2. _____

3. _____

Identify five specific language choices you made in preparing for one of your classroom speech/presentations:

1. _____

2. _____

3. _____

4. _____

5. _____

Identify three language considerations you will keep in mind for your persuasive speeches because you have become more aware of language choices as both a speaker and a listener.

1. _____

2. _____

3. _____

LISTENING

Complete the assessment below. Then write what you learned about your listening in your communication journal.

Listening Self-Assessment

1. Whom do you think listens most effectively to you (e.g., parent, friend, teacher, sibling)?

_____

2. How do you know this person is listening effectively (e.g., asks questions, rephrases my ideas, nods head, makes eye contact)?

_____

3. To whom do you listen most effectively (e.g., parent, teacher, friend, sibling)?

_____

4. Why do you listen effectively to this person (e.g., she/he listens to me, the topics discussed, our relationship, respect)?

_____

5. What communication skill do you admire most about your friends (e.g., speaking, listening, writing, reading)? Why?

_____

6. How do you respond when you are listening effectively (e.g., eye contact, facial expression, forward lean, nod head, ask questions, rephrase message)?

_____

7. What distracts you most from listening to another person in a conversation (e.g., other person's voice, speech rate or appearance; topic; own interest or preoccupation; no purpose for listening)?

_____

8. When you are at home, how often do you converse with your parent(s) and/or entire family for at least a 15-minute duration (e.g., every day, twice a week, once a week, seldom)?

_____

9. In your 15 minute–plus conversations with your family, what percentage of the time do you listen?

_____

Classroom Lecture Listening Questionnaire

Communicators

1. What single personal or communicative characteristic of an instructor most influences your listening to her/his lecture?

   _____

2. What single personal characteristic or condition of your own most influences your listening to the teacher's lecture?

   _____

3. What single physical behavior or response on your part enables you to listen effectively to a classroom lecture?

   _____

Message

1. What single goal or objective of the message causes you to listen to a classroom lecture?

   _____

2. What single characteristic of the lecture material or information motivates you to listen to a classroom lecture?

   _____

Means of Communicating

1. What single thing can an instructor do to supplement what she/he says and help you listen more effectively?

   _____

2. Do you comprehend material best when presented visually or orally?

   _____

Communication Context

1. What single classroom factor most influences your listening to a lecture?

   _____

2. What is the maximum length of time that you can effectively listen to a lecture?

   _____

3. What time of day do you most effectively listen to classroom lectures?

   _____

4. Where in the classroom would you sit for most effective listening?

   _____

MEDIA LITERACY

1. One important part of youth entertainment culture is videogames. Some contend that video games generate more revenue for media organizations than blockbuster films. Unfortunately, not enough attention is paid to looking at the games in terms of cultural texts. An interesting writing activity for students is to ask them to perform a content analysis of a videogame. Ask them to identify and comment on the following aspects of a videogame they choose or you assign.

   a. What is the name of the game? What does the name tell you about the content? Does it have positive or negative meanings or connotations?

   b. How do you score points in the videogame? Is it through a violent activity such as shooting, stabbing, or the killing of characters? Do you earn points in other ways?

   c. Does the game have a rating? What is it? What does the rating mean?

   d. Who is the target audience for the game? (teenage boys, teenage girls, etc.) Try to be as specific as possible.

   e. What type of physical skill is required to play the game? Can you get better with practice? Does speed matter?

   f. On a scale of 1 (lowest) to 10 (highest) how lifelike are the images? How does this affect your experience when playing?

   g. Ask students to read the "warnings" on the insert brochure. Why does the videogame have "warnings"? Have you ever experienced the side effects described? Do you know anyone who has experienced side effects from videogame playing? If there were not real side effects, why would the manufacturer use warnings?

   h. Do you think videogame playing can be addictive? Why or why not?

   i. What type of effects, if any, does playing the game have on the player (desensitization to violence, increased focus, better eye–hand coordination, etc.)?

2. The Academy Awards® honor media producers, actors, and creators for outstanding work in theatrically released motion pictures. The purposes of this activity are to encourage students to understand the collaborative nature of producing media products, to recognize those films that are considered "best in class" and understand why. Aesthetic appreciation of motion pictures encourages students to watch films more critically.

   a. Ask students to watch the Academy Awards® program. Have them identify the different awards given (acting, special effects, makeup, costume, etc.) and to whom the award was given. Discuss in class.

   b. Using the categories provided by the Academy, assign students to small groups (preferably each group should be assigned to see a film that has won an award). In their groups, ask students to work as a collaborative team to identify specific instances in the film that highlight the most representative exemplars of the category assigned. Have students explain why scenes were selected, what they liked/did not like, and why.

   c. Students will present their reactions to the film as a group, including their analysis about the category to which they were assigned. Students should perform research about their category (e.g. costumes, make-up, sound, etc.). This may involve information about the history of the film or the award winners, for example. Encourage students to incorporate advertisements, articles, promotional materials, Web site information, or props. Remind students that their presentation needs to be collaboratively planned and executed (much like the film they have viewed).

3. Ask students to identify their favorite celebrity. In class, discuss the concept of celebrity. What does it mean to be a celebrity? Do celebrities have a responsibility to their fans or to society? Why or why not? Ask students to research the history of the individual they have identified. Assign a paper in which students must compare and contrast a contemporary media celebrity (assigned or student selected) to a popular historic figure (preferably one studied in class). Consider the following questions:

   a. What differences and similarities exist?

   b. If the historic figure were alive today, would he/she be considered a celebrity? Why or why not?

   c. What basic principles/morals/ethics does each man/woman stand for/promote?

   d. Does the individual represent the culture/era in which they are/were popular? How?